BURMA

HUTCHINSON'S UNIVERSITY LIBRARY

BRITISH EMPIRE HISTORY

EDITOR:

SIR REGINALD COUPLAND

K.C.M.G., C.I.E., M.A., D.LITT.

*Late Beit Professor of the History of the British Empire
in the University of Oxford*

BURMA

by

D. G. E. HALL

M.A., D.LIT., F.R.HIST.S.

PROFESSOR OF THE HISTORY OF SOUTH-EAST
ASIA IN THE UNIVERSITY OF LONDON

FORMERLY PROFESSOR OF HISTORY
IN THE UNIVERSITY OF RANGOON

LONDON
HUTCHINSON'S UNIVERSITY LIBRARY

Hutchinson's University Library

178-202 Great Portland Street, London, W.1

London   Melbourne   Sydney   Auckland
Bombay Johannesburg New York Toronto

First published 1950
Second edition 1956

Printed in Great Britain
by The Anchor Press, Ltd.,
Tiptree, Essex

CONTENTS

NOTE ON PRONUNCIATION

(i) As Burmese was originally a monosyllabic language its proper names are usually combinations of two or more words, e.g. Kyauk-sè, stone weir; Myit-kyi-na, river-great-near; Ye-nan-gyaung, water-stinking-creek. For correct pronunciation therefore they must be correctly split up into syllables. Syllables are either (*a*) open or (*b*) terminate with nasalized -*n* or -*ng* after a vowel or (*c*) terminate with -*t* or -*k* used as glottal stops, not as consonants pronounced with an explosion as in English.

(ii) So far as consonants at the beginning of syllables are concerned Burmese makes a clear distinction between aspirated and unaspirated ones. The English system of transliteration shows an aspirated consonant by placing '*h*' before it, e.g. *hk-*, *hl-*, *hm-*, *hs-*, *ht-*, etc.

(iii) It should also be noted that

   ng- is nasalized in the same way as at the end of a syllable,
   ky- is pronounced 'ch',
   gy- is pronounced 'j',
   g- is pronounced as in 'good', never as in 'germ'.

(iv) Vowels are pronounced as in Italian.

(v) There are the following diphthongs:

   ou or *au* pronounced as in 'bough', never as in 'taught',
   aw pronounced as in 'law',
   ei pronounced as in 'eight',
   ai pronounced as 'i' in 'like'.

(vi) N.B.—The pronunciation of the following nasalized vowels:

   an like 'ah-n',
   in as in English,
   on as in 'own', never as in 'on',
   un as in 'put', never as in 'bun'.

(vii) In common English usage:

   Chiengmai is pronounced Cheng-mai.
   Pegu is pronounced Pee-gew.
   Moulmein is pronounced Mool-mein.
   In Maymyo and Mandalay the '*ay*' sound is as in English.
   Prome has one syllable only.
   Bassein and Insein are pronounced Basseen and Inseen.

CHAPTER I

THE PRE-PAGAN PERIOD

THE early history of Burma is obscure. The Burmese chronicles begin with the supposed foundation of Tagaung in 850 B.C., but the stories they tell are copies of Indian legends taken from Sanskrit or Pali originals. The earliest extant description of Further India is in the Geography of the Alexandrian scholar, Ptolemy, who flourished in the middle of the second century A.D. He refers to the inhabitants of the Irrawaddy Delta as cannibals. These were not, however, the Burmese, for their migrations into the country had not started. In Ptolemy's time the dominant race in Indo-China was Indonesian. It must have been strongly represented in Burma, since her modern inhabitants show clear traces of the mixture.

Buddhist legends point to Indian influence coming by sea. There is the story of the two brothers, Tapusa and Palikat, who visited Gautama and received from him eight hairs of his head, which they are said to have brought to Burma and enshrined beneath the Shwe Dagon Pagoda. The Mon chronicles contain the story of Sona and Uttara, said to have been deputed to the 'golden land', Suvarna Bhumi, by the Third Buddhist Council at Pataliputra c. 241 B.C. Was Burma the 'golden land' of the *jatakas*, or birth stories of the Buddha?

Actually, the fragments of the Pali scriptures found on the site of the Pyu capital of Śrī Kṣetra constitute the earliest evidence of Indian culture in Burma. And they do not date earlier than 500 A.D. Chinese writers of the third century A.D., however, refer to a Buddhist kingdom of Lin-yang, which Gordon Luce, the authority for this period, places in central Burma. Later Chinese writings, from the fourth century onwards, mention a people in central Burma, the P'iao, among whom 'prince and minister, father and son, elder and younger each have their order of precedence'. By Chinese standards a civilized people, it would seem. These were the Pyu, the ruins of whose capital at Old Prome, Śrī Kṣetra or 'Field of

Glory', with its massive circular city walls and traces of broad moats, can still be seen.

The Pyu were the earliest inhabitants of Burma of whom records are extant. Inscriptions in their language using a South Indian script have been found as far north as Halingyi in Shwebo district, but mostly at old Prome. They show a Vikrama dynasty ruling there at least from 673 to 718, which is thought to have inaugurated the Burmese Era beginning in March A.D. 638. There is mention of another dynasty with an Indian name, the Varman line, ruling over a neighbouring and rival city, but Old Prome is the only Pyu site so far to be excavated in that area. Outside its walls are three stupas of archaic type, of which the Bawbawgyi, a cylinder of plastered brick 150 feet high, with a hollow shaft in the centre, crowned with a flattened cone, is the best-preserved. Of particular interest are the small vaulted chapels, of brick and arched in the style of the Pagan temples of which they are prototypes.

Religious remains show both forms of Buddhism, Mahayanism and Hinayanism, together with Vishnu worship. There are large stone Buddhist sculptures in relief in the Gupta style, bronze statuettes of Avalokitesvara, one of the three chief Mahayanist Bodhisattvas, and so many stone sculptures of Vishnu that the city was sometimes referred to as 'Vishnu City'. The people burnt their dead and stored the ashes in urns, hundreds of which have been discovered. Their language survives only in inscriptions. It seems to have been related to Burmese; it is monosyllabic, and has a tonal system for which dots are used as symbols. For what little is known of it we are indebted to the late Dr. Otto Blagden, who by a comparison of the four faces of the Myazedi inscription of Pagan (A.D. 1113), where the same text appears in Pyu, Mon, Burmese and Pali, established the meanings of between fifty and 100 words.

So far as Arakan is concerned, the inscriptions show traces of two early dynasties holding sway in the north. The earlier one, a Candra dynasty, seems to have been founded in the middle of the fourth century A.D. Its capital was known by the Indian name of Vaisali and it maintained close connections with India. Thirteen kings of this dynasty are said to have reigned for a total period of 230 years. The second dynasty was founded in the eighth century by a ruler referred to as Sri Dharmavijaya, who was of pure Kṣatriya descent. His grandson married a daughter of the Pyu king of Śrī Kṣetra.

In about the year 760 Kolofeng, the second king of the powerful T'ai kingdom of Nanchao, which occupied the West and North-West of Yunnan, conquered the Pyu kingdom. Allied with the Tibetans against China, and anxious to secure his communications with the West, he decided that it was necessary to control the valley of the Upper Irrawaddy. He built a fortress to control the tribes of the Irrawaddy plain, and enlisted some of them in his armies. His successor, I-mou-hsun, on concluding peace with China, sent a troupe of musicians, including Pyu, to the Chinese court. They appeared there early in 800. Two years later a formal Pyu embassy, led by Shunanto, son of a chieftain referred to as Yung Chiang by the Chinese, accompanied a mission from Nanchao to Hsi-nan-fu. The songs and dances of the Pyu so delighted the Imperial Secretary, Po Chü-i, that he composed a poem in honour of the occasion. It begins:

Music from the land of P'iao, music from the land of P'iao!
Brought hither from the great ocean's south-west corner.
Yung Ch'iang's son Shunant'o
Has come with an offering of southern tunes to fête the New Year.
Our Emperor has taken his seat in the courtyard of the Palace.

A dance is presented; when it ends the Council of State advises the Emperor

That such an occasion as an Emperor watching the P'iao presenting new tunes
Ought to be recorded in the state annals, to be handed down to future generations.

But an old farmer, hoeing the earth, sings a different song, counselling the monarch to heal the sufferings of his subjects rather than listen to P'iao music, and the poem ends

Music of the P'iao, in vain you raise your din.
Better were it that my lord should listen to that peasant's
humble words.

At the time of these embassies it would seem that the Pyu
capital had been transferred north to Halingyi. The Chinese
histories describe it as surrounded by a brick wall of green enamel
protected by a brick-lined moat. It had twelve gates and was
fortified by towers at the corners. The city contained a hundred
Buddhist monasteries, decorated with gold, silver and multi-
coloured paintings and hung with embroidered cloths. Near the
palace was a gigantic image of a white elephant before which all
litigants had to kneel and reflect upon the justice or injustice of
their cases. In time of public distress the king would prostrate
himself before the elephant, burning incense and confessing his
sins. Boys and girls were accustomed to live in monasteries
from the age of seven until their twentieth year studying the
Buddhist faith.

The Pyu kingdom came to a sudden end in 832, when rebellious Nanchao tribes plundered its capital and deported
thousands of captives to Yunnan Fu. Of what subsequently
happened to the Pyu people there is no record. There came a
time when they lost not only their language but even their
separate identity as a people. Were they a very early wave of
Burmese immigration, the advance guard some centuries ahead
of the main invasion? There is much to commend this view.
Burmese tradition seems to support it, since it claims that in
the earliest times the Burmese people were divided into three
main tribes, the Pyu, the Kanran and the Thet.

The Pyu had claimed suzerainty over eighteen subject
kingdoms, mainly in southern Burma. Among them were the
kingdom of Mi-chen, destroyed by Nanchao in 835, the *k'un-lun*
states of K'un-lang, and Lu-yu near a port Mo-ti-po, from
which, it is said, Palembang and Java could be reached. The
word *k'un-lun* refers to the Mons, called Talaings by the
Burmese, a people of Mongoloid type, who inhabited the Delta
of the Irrawaddy, and had absorbed Indian culture and
Hinayana Buddhism. The centre of their power was the
kingdom of Dvaravati in southern Siam, which controlled a

part of Tenasserim, while to the north it had colonized Lamphun (Haripunjaya). The Nanchao attacks, which had overwhelmed the Pyu and Mi-chen, were beaten off by the Mons. An offshoot of the Khmer Empire of Cambodia, whose monuments remain today some of the noblest expressions of human artistic genius, their states in the triangle between Lamphun and the Gulfs of Siam and Martaban maintained close contact with each other and developed a civilization, which in due course came to exercise a powerful influence upon the Burmese themselves.

Arab geographers mention the Mon country of Lower Burma under the name of Raman'n'adesa. The earliest reference is in the *Book of Routes and of Provinces* by Ibn Khordadzebeh (844–48). He tells us that the king possesses 50,000 elephants and that the country produces cotton, velvet stuffs and aloes wood. At this period the centre of gravity of the Mon kingdom shifted towards the west and it is interesting to note that of the various dates given in different chronicles for the foundation of the city of Pegu the tradition ascribing it to the year 825 is preferred by historical scholarship.

So far as reliable records are concerned, the period from the middle of the ninth to the middle of the eleventh centuries is a blank. This is all the more unfortunate since it was during this period that the Burmese entered Burma. Their original home seems to have been somewhere in the north-west of China, probably Kansu, between the Gobi Desert and north-east Tibet. The earliest Chinese written records, coming from the latter half of the second millennium B.C., call them the Ch'iang. Chinese hostility forced them to take refuge in north-east Tibet. In the first millennium B.C. they were pursued by the Chinese rulers of Ts'in through the mountains towards the south. There we lose sight of them for a long period until they reappear many centuries later among the Mang tribes under the suzerainty of Nanchao. To escape from the dominance of Nanchao they entered the plains of Burma, coming down through the region between the 'Nmai Hka and the Salween and ultimately settling in the Kyaukse district. Kansu, their earliest recorded home, if one dare be definite on this point, possessed in late Neolithic times a civilization possibly higher

than that of the rest of China. It produced the finest painted
pottery yet discovered among Neolithic remains. Much of this
culture must have been lost by the ancestors of the Burmese
during their long trek to the south.

The influence of Nanchao gave the Burmese many charac-
teristic features, such as the use of the water-buffalo, the
terrace-cultivation of hill slopes and their system of wet rice-
cultivation in the plains. In addition they learnt the arts of war
and the breeding of horses. South-west Yunnan, their home
while under Nanchao, was a great breeding-place for horses,
and they became so famous as breeders that in northern Burma
and as far as Manipur the horse is still referred to as 'the
foreign' or the 'Burmese animal'. Then from mountaineers
living on the cold highlands they had to become lowlanders,
living in the torrid heat of the dry zone of central Burma. They
seized the Kyauksè area from the Mons, who had built an
irrigation system and cultivated the area intensively. The
Ledwin, 'the rice-country', as the Burmese came to call it
later, when they had improved the Mon irrigation system and
made the district the 'economic key of the north country', was
right from the start, significantly enough the base from which
they developed their political control over the rest of the land.

The Ledwin was not their only acquisition from the Mons.
The evidence goes to show that long before Anawrahta's conquest of Thaton in 1057, traditionally held to have signalized
the beginning of Mon influence, those isolated in the north by
the Burmese thrust into Kyauksè had taught their masters to
read and write. They also introduced Buddhism to the Burmese
and much else besides, if the many words of Mon origin now
found in the Burmese language are any indication.

From their Kyauksè base the Burmese spread out in
several directions. West of the Irrawaddy they seized another
oasis in what is now Minbu district, where they took over an even
older canal-system. Downstream they made their way to the
Taungdwingyi ricelands and Prome. Northwards they spread
to Shwebo, Tabayin and Myedu. They made settlements up
the Chindwin. One wave of them reached the Pondaung
Range and the Chin Hills, and ultimately Akyab in northern
Arakan. At what period of time the national name, *Mranma*,

i.e. the Burmans, first came into use, it is impossible to say. In Burmese the word first appears in an inscription of 1190. A Mon inscription of about 1102 refers to them as the *Mirma*. The name by which the Chinese knew them, *Mien*, presumably representing the first syllable of *Mranma*, is first mentioned in 1273.

The religion of the Burmese, before they adopted Buddhism, was animism. Not only was it prevalent throughout Indo-china and Indonesia at the time, but its universal persistence in these regions, notwithstanding the spread of Brahmanism, Buddhism and Mohammedanism, makes it still today a factor of prime importance in the religious outlook of the various peoples. Burmese animism is made up of the worship of a host of spirits called *nats*. Usually they were, and are, local nature gods, the spirits of earth and sky, rain and wind, whirlpool and whirlwind, of mountains, rivers and trees, of the jungle, and even of villages and houses. The stories told of them show that the more famous ones were believed to be the disembodied spirits of human beings, raised to the rank of *nats* through noble deeds or great suffering. The national religious festivals of today were all originally animist, and even when adopted into the Buddhist calendar lost none of their pre-Buddhist significance. Thus the New Year water festival, *Thingyan*, celebrated the annual return of the Thagya Min, or King of the Spirit World, to the earth. And although the *Thadingyut* festival of light, which ends the Buddhist Lent in September or October, commemorates the legend of Gautama ascending into spiritland to expound the Law to his mother, who had become Queen of the *Nats*, it is a clear case of a Buddhist legend being grafted on to a pre-Buddhist practice. Ceremonies to propitiate the *nats* were connected with every phase of life from birth to death, from ploughing to harvesting, and along with them went the use of charms of every kind from those which ensured sound sleep at night to those which conferred invulnerability in battle. Almost all have survived down to the present day, the commonest being the practice of tattooing adolescent boys from the waist downwards with elaborate designs of demons, dragons, peacocks, fish, quails, cats and flying animals.

CHAPTER II

THE PAGAN PERIOD (1044-1287)

THE ruins of the city of Pagan, on the eastern bank of the Irrawaddy about 120 miles south of Mandalay, are the most impressive relics of the first period of Burmese greatness. They cover a river front of nearly twenty miles to a depth of five miles inland. In this area the remains of no less than 5000 temples and pagodas may still be seen. Originally there are said to have been no less than 13,000 Buddhist shrines and monasteries in and around the city. It is one of the richest archaeological sites in the Indo-Chinese peninsula.

The traditional date of the foundation of Pagan is 849. The chronicles claim that in that year a chief named Pyanpya enclosed the city with a wall, the remains of which may still be seen in the Sarabha Gate. The earliest occurrence of the name is, oddly enough, in a Cham inscription of the first half of the eleventh century. Here it is rendered *Pukam*. In Burma its earliest mention is in an Old Mon inscription of 1093. The inscriptions usually refer to it by its classical name of Arimaddana, 'trampler on enemies'. They call the kingdom *Tambradipa*, 'land of copper', and the region *Tattadesa*, 'the parched country'. Incidentally they have nothing to say about Pyanpya; the only Burmese king mentioned in them before Anawrahta is Saw Rahan, whose stronghold was at Mount Turan, eight miles east of Pagan.

The founder of the greatness of Pagan was Anawrahta (1044-1077). He was the first king of Burma and with him Burmese history proper begins. Trustworthy historical material concerning his reign is meagre. Epigraphy is the only reliable source and as yet it has been inadequately studied. In the chronicles he is a majestic and romantic figure who gains his throne by slaying a usurper in single combat. Many are the stories told of him, but they contain so much that is legendary that it is wellnigh impossible to distinguish between fact and fiction. The traditional version of his reign can best be studied in Pe Maung Tin and Luce's delightful translation of the *Glass Palace Chronicle.*

Anawrahta's reign was one of conquests through which he united most of Burma under his sway. To the west he crossed the Arakan Yoma and forced northern Arakan to acknowledge his overlordship. He planned to bring back to his capital the huge Mahamuni image at Dinnyawadi in Akyab district; but the task was too great for his resources, and he contented himself with desecrating the shrine, to prevent its magical figures and trees from assisting Arakanese raids into Burma. To the east he expanded his control up to the foothills of the Shan mountains, planting outposts in strong points to mark the boundary, and exacting tokens of allegiance from the chiefs beyond. The chronicles of the T'ai states of the Upper Menam assert that he led a campaign into Nanchao as far as Talifu to obtain a tooth-relic of the Buddha. He is also said to have attacked the Cambodian Empire and to have ruled over most of the present territory of Siam. Burmese sources, however, make no such claims on his behalf, and the stories must be regarded as apocryphal.

Anawrahta's most important conquests were in the south. Tradition has it that he was visited by a famous Hinayana teacher of Lower Burma, Shin Arahan, under whose influence he sought to purify his realm of Mahayanist practices, and break the power of the Ari priesthood at Thamati. The Ari are said to have taught magic formulae which released sinners from the operation of the law of *karma*, and to have exercised the *jus primae noctis*. Scholars have tried to associate their name with the prevailing *naga* worship and Tantric practices, but the word seems only to indicate dwellers in jungle monasteries. Anawrahta broke their power, but the sect was never suppressed.

The work of purification could make little progress for lack of the sacred books of Buddhism. Far away in the south the Mon Kingdom of Thaton, which had adopted its Buddhism from Conjeveram in South India, possessed thirty complete sets of the Tripitaka, the 'Three Baskets of the Law'. Shin Arahan persuaded his royal master to apply for one of them. The request was rejected with insults, so the story goes, and Anawrahta in a great campaign by land and water captured

Thaton and deported to his northern capital its entire population of 30,000 souls, including the king and his court and all
the clergy. The sacred scriptures were borne by no less than
thirty-two white elephants, we are told. At Pagan a special
library building, the Tripitakataik, was erected to house them.
Directed by Shin Arahan, Mon monks spread far and wide the
doctrine of Hinayana Buddhism. Pali, the language of the
Tripitakas, became the sacred language of the Burmese. The
Mon alphabet was adopted, and Burmese became for the first
time a written, not merely a spoken language.

The conquest of Thaton in 1057 was a decisive event in
Burmese history. It brought the Burman into direct contact
with the Indian civilizing influences in the south and opened
the way for intercourse with Buddhist centres overseas, especially Ceylon. The possession of the Pali scriptures revolutionized his outlook: they supplied him 'ready-made, with a
complete mental outfit' (Luce). They introduced him to the
Buddhist ethic, which, as monasteries and teachers multiplied
throughout the land, began to exert its moral force, to restrain
his more barbarous impulses, and to liberate him from the
worst of his animistic practices.

But let it not be thought that Anawrahta and Shin Arahan
brought back pure Hinayana Buddhism from Thaton as the
chronicles assert. The evidence of the inscriptions, Luce warns
us, shows that the Buddhism of Pagan 'was mixed up with
Hindu Brahmanic cults, Vaisnavism in particular. It was tinged
with Mahayanism, and towards the end of the dynasty at least
with Tantrism. It rested doubtless on a deep bed of Naga and
Nat worship.'[1] And it is interesting to note that the throne-
room, built for himself by the captive King Manuha of Thaton
in the Nanpaya shrine at Myinkaba, south of Pagan, and still
in existence, contains bas-reliefs of Hindu deities, "so
prominent", says Harvey, "as to leave no room for doubt that
Thaton Buddhism was largely Hindu".[2] Hinayana Buddhism
has subsequently made great strides toward eliminating these
extraneous elements. But it still retains traces of Brahmanism,

[1] Luce, G. H., 'Burma's Debt to Pagan', *Journal of the Burma Research
Society*, Vol. XXII, p. 121.
[2] Harvey, G. E., *History of Burma*, p. 28.

and in addition to the Nat worship which it has assimilated there remains today a distinctive animistic religion, which has no connection whatever with Buddhism and is frowned on by the monkhood.

One of the most famous stories connected with Nat worship purports to come from the reign of Anawrahta. It relates to the ancient custom of burying alive a human sacrifice beneath the foundations of an important building in order to provide it with a guardian spirit. At the foot of Kyauksè Hill near Mandalay are two huge boulders called the Brother and Sister. Tradition asserts that when the king was at work on the Kyauksè irrigation system, it was decided to bury a victim under each weir. One of his queens, the sister of the Shan chief Myodyi, asked that her death should suffice for all. Her sacrifice was accepted, and she became the tutelary goddess of all the weirs. Her brother, who considered himself Anawrahta's equal, was summoned to pay homage. Rather than involve his people in war, he set out to obey the summons. At the border, however, overcome with shame, he threw himself into the Zawgyi river and was drowned. Thereupon brother and sister became *nats* inhabiting the two boulders, and to this day are objects of widespread worship in upper Burma.

It may be that the most important result of the conquest of the south was the opening of a window to the sea. Still, Mon civilization was higher than Burmese, and for a century after the fall of Thaton Mon cultural influence predominated at Pagan. It had also begun to show itself strongly in Khmer architecture. Suryavarman I (1002-50) was one of Angkor's great builders. His two most famous buildings, the Phimeanakas and the Ta Keo, display marked Mon characteristics. Actually none of the great temples of the Pagan period dates from Anawrahta's reign. He built solid pagodas, not temples. His principal one, the Shwezigon, was erected over Buddhist relics from Prome and Ceylon; it is surrounded by shrines dedicated to the Thirty-seven Nats, crude and barbaric in design and execution. His buildings are childish in comparison with the artistic and technical standards of the Ananda and the Thatpyinnyu, whose affinities are with Khmer architecture.

B

Nevertheless, although it is not until a later reign, that of Kyanzittha (1084–1112), that the effects of the new cultural connection with the outer world begin clearly to appear, a story in the chronicles indicates that in Anawrahta's own lifetime at least one important overseas contact was established. A king of Ceylon, Vijaya Bahu I, forced to defend his kingdom and his religion against the attacks of the Hindu Cholas of the Carnatic, sought his help. Anawrahta sent a costly present, but no troops. Vijaya Bahu, however, managed to drive out the invaders. Thereupon he again sent envoys to Pagan asking for monks and scriptures to aid him in the task of reconstruction. These were despatched, and as a token of gratitude he sent Anawrahta a miraculously produced replica of the famous Buddha Tooth of Kandy. It was received with the highest honours and placed in a jewelled casket under the Shwezigon Pagoda.

Intercourse with Ceylon tended to have a marked effect upon the history of Burmese Buddhism. Burmese tradition asserts that in A.D. 403 the scriptures were brought to Thaton from Ceylon by the apostle Buddhaghosa. Modern research, however, connects Thaton Buddhism with the important Hinayana school at Conjeveram, which flourished under the commentator Dhammapala in the fifth century. It was apparently from this source that the Mons acquired the Pallava alphabet with which they wrote their earliest inscriptions. At the time when the Pagan kings began to develop relations with Ceylon, Brahmanism had triumphed over Buddhism at Conjeveram, and Ceylon was coming to take its place as the main Hinayana centre.

When Anawrahta died in 1077 his rule extended over the greater part of Burma proper, northern Arakan and northern Tennasserim, while a number of Shan chieftains in the mountainous regions to the east of central Burma acknowledged his suzerainty. His achievements left a permanent impression upon his country and people. His son Sawlu (1077–84), who succeeded him, was so incompetent that it says much for the genius of the father that his kingdom survived the test. The main danger was in the south, where the Mons rebelled, captured the feeble king, murdered him and threatened Pagan itself. It looked as if it was now the turn of the Burmese to be conquered by the Mons. Sawlu's half-brother Kyanzittha, however, routed the Mons and became the third ruler of the dynasty. He was enthroned at Pagan with majestic ceremonial. Later he erected a whole series of inscriptions, which bear eloquent witness to the splendour of his conceptions. "King Kyanzittha shall sit upon a throne of gold adorned with gems, and he shall enjoy the splendour of royalty", runs one sentence from the great inscription at the Shwezigon Pagoda. It is in the Mon language, as are most of his inscriptions, and their literary standard is high. Mon scholarship was still well ahead of Burmese. Morover Kyanzittha devoted special attention to the Mons, whose revolt had so nearly wrecked the monarchy. His main political object was to unify the diverse peoples composing his realm.

Of increasing contacts with the outer world his reign provides much evidence. He was the first of his house to send missions to China, probably with the intention of facilitating overland trade with Yunnan, which appears to have revived after Nanchao became tributary to China at the end of the ninth century. His first mission, in 1103, is the first Burmese embassy to be recorded in the *History of the Song*. When his second mission appeared in 1106, the Council of Rites laid down that it was to be accorded the same honours as were accustomed to be shown to the envoys of the Arab princes or of Tongking. This incident shows how much the prestige of the Burmese kingdom had grown in the sixty-two years since its foundation.

A Mon inscription at the Shwehsandaw Pagoda at Prome shows that Kyanzittha was also the first king of Burma to undertake the restoration of the Mahabodi Temple at Buddhagaya, the most sacred place in the Buddhist world, commemorating, as it does, the attainment of enlightenment by Gautama beneath the shade of its holy tree. "Thereafter," runs the inscription, "many persons from all the provinces came into his presence to attend him." One of these was a Chola prince to whom he had written a pious message "concerning the grace of the Jewel of the Lord, the Jewel of His Law, and the Jewel of His Clergy, with vermilion ink upon a leaf of gold". Extensive maritime trade with Indo-China had been developed by the Chola dynasty in the Carnatic. They had also raided the Malay empire of Srivijaya. It has been suggested that the prince

was the ruler of a Tamil colony in the Delta region and that
Anawrahta's conquest of the south had really been undertaken
to forestall a possible Chola invasion. These are mere guesses:
there is no evidence that the prince was anything else than a
traveller paying a social visit.

Kyanzittha's supreme monument is the Ananda Temple.
The story goes that Buddhist monks from India described the
great cave temple of Ananta at Udayagiri in Orissa to the king
and kindled his zeal to build one in imitation. Duroiselle, however, is of the opinion that the temple of Paharpur in northern
Bengal may have served as the model. Built of brick covered with
stucco the main structure is a square mass, from which rise six
successively diminishing terraces up to a spire with the bulging
shape of a central Indian temple, and surmounted by the
tapering pinnacle crowned with a gilded *hti* which characterizes
the Burmese pagoda. From its four sides large gabled vestibules
project in such a way as to make the ground-plan a perfect
Greek cross. The interior consists of lofty vaulted corridors,
concentric in plan, leading to four central chambers, in each of
which stands a colossal image of the Buddha, some thirty feet
high, facing the entrance porch. The head and shoulders of the
statue are lit by natural light from an unseen source far above
the spectator's head, so as to produce a dazzling effect as one
passes up the dim corridor. Before the western image two
life-size kneeling statues represent the founder, Kyanzittha,
and the monk, Shin Arahan. In the galleries running round
the outside of the building are 1500 plaques illustrating the
jataka legends of earlier incarnations of the Buddha. Inside the
corridors are eighty niches containing sculptures representing
scenes from his own life. All are the work of Indian craftsmen
and many are of high artistic merit. Externally there is much
fanciful ornamentation to roofs, gables, windows and door-
ways. Less imposing than the Angkor Wat in Cambodia or the
Borobudur in Java, the Ananda nonetheless has an air of light-
ness and delicate beauty in its way unsurpassable; and when
seen from a distance in the rays of the early morning sun,
presents an unforgettable loveliness.

When Kyanzittha lay dying in 1112 at the age of seventy, his
only son, so the story goes, made ceremonial offerings at the

Myazedi Pagoda, south of Pagan. These he recorded in the quadrilingual inscription already referred to in the previous chapter. The discovery of this important pillar in 1911 provided the key not only to the Pyu language but also to the chronology of the early Pagan kings, which till then had been doubtful.

Kyanzittha's successor was Alaungsithu (1112-1167), the son of his daughter and of Sawlu's son, Sawyun. The new king's early years were spent repressing revolts, especially in Tenasserim and north Arakan. A Pali inscription found at Mergui is evidence that Tenasserim then paid allegiance to the Pagan monarchy. In north Arakan a usurper had driven out the rightful heir, who had fled to Pagan, where he subsequently died. His son, with Alaungsithu's assistance, recovered the inheritance, and was charged by the Burmese king to discharge his debt by repairing the Buddhagaya shrine. An inscription, still to be seen there, tells of the mission which he sent for the purpose; and it is noteworthy that the basement images and other details of the temple are Burmese in style.

Alaungsithu travelled far and wide throughout his dominions building many works of merit; these pious pilgrimages form the main theme of the chronicles of his reign. But he neglected the work of administration, and there was apparently much disorder during his long absences from the capital. His zeal for religion found its highest expression in the noble Thatpyinnyu Temple consecrated in 1144. It stands about 500 yards from the Ananda, and with its spire rising to a height of over 200 feet from the ground is the tallest of all the Pagan monuments. Its style is similar to that of the Ananda, but there is a much greater elevation of the mass before the tapering process begins, and the position of the main shrine is thus high above the ground.

Our matter-of-fact age would today condemn a ruler who neglected the pedestrian task of administration in order to concentrate on 'useless' temple-building. But such an attitude of mind fails to grasp the 'otherworldliness' of the Buddhist ideal, which inspired these works of merit. Its spirit is manifest in Luce's glowing translation of Alaungsithu's Pali prayer inscribed in the Shwegu Pagoda:

> But I would build a causeway sheer athwart
> The river of Samsara (illusion), and all folk
> Would speed across thereby until they reach
> The Blessed City. I myself would cross
> And drag the drowning over. Ay, myself
> Tamed, I would tame the wilful; comforted,
> Comfort the timid; wakened, wake the asleep;
> Cool, cool the burning; freed, set free the bound.
> Tranquil and led by the good doctrines I
> Would hatred calm. The three immoral states,
> Greed, hate, delusion, rooted all in self,
> O may they die, whe never born in me.

The noblest minds of Pagan felt the fascination of Buddhism much as those of mediaeval Europe that of Christianity; reverence for the Religion and its Founder absorbed their whole being.

In his old age Alaungsithu fell a victim to a court intrigue engineered by three of his sons. One of them, Narathu, murdered his father and seized the throne. His short reign, 1167–70, was a time of disorder and bloodshed, during which Shin Arahan's successor, Panthagu, left the country in disgust and retired to Ceylon. In feverish atonement for his many cruelties Narathu built the largest of all the Pagan temples, the Dammayan. Its ground-plan is the same as that of the Ananda, and its brick-work of a high order; but artistically it is far below the standard of its two predecessors. And it failed to earn for its founder the pardon he sought, for he was violently done to death before he had reigned three years.

His son Naratheinhka, who succeeded him, failed completely to deal with the anarchy which was widespread throughout the land. He was murdered by rebels in 1173. Then his younger brother, Narapatisithu, came to the throne, and during his reign of thirty-seven years (1173–1210) there is little record of disorder and much of building. The list of his foundations is imposing, and includes two of the finest temples at Pagan, the Gawdawpalin and the Sulamani, besides innumerable pagodas in many parts of the realm. Narapatisithu also promoted much irrigation work in the Kyauksè and Shwebo districts. An attempt to construct irrigation canals in the Minbu district proved a failure. It was believed that Thagyamin, the King of the Spirits, was opposed to the project, and, centuries later, when the English irrigated the area, the tradition was still so powerful that many cultivators at first refused to apply for land. Narapatisithu's most important work was the construction of the famous stone weir from which Kyaukse takes its name.

The Buddhist religion seems to have suffered severely during the six years of anarchy before Narapatisithu's accession. In 1173 Panthagu returned from Ceylon. He was a very old man and lived only a short time after his return. There were many who felt that Theravada Buddhism in Burma needed revivifying, and their enthusiasm for reform must have been fanned by his accounts of Sinhalese Buddhism. Thus it came about that in 1180 his successor as Head of the Order, the Mon Uttarajiva, went with a large company of monks to seek fresh spiritual strength in Ceylon, and a new chapter opened in the religious history of Burma.

Monks, returning from Ceylon with new notions and practices, refused to accept the validity of Thaton-Buddhism ordination. The quarrel became a schism; those who derived their ordination from Shin Arahan were known as the Former Order, those who derived it from Ceylon as the Latter Order. The king encouraged the new movement. More and more clergy were sent to Ceylon, where they received ordination at the ancient Mahavihara Monastery. But the older form did not yield easily: the schism lasted two centuries before Conjeveram Buddhism finally died out.

Narapatisithu's son Nantaungmya, who followed him to the throne in 1210, is better known by his nickname Htilominlo, 'he whom the umbrella wished to be king'. He was supposed to have been miraculously indicated as his father's successor by the royal white umbrella. He was king in name only. He devoted himself entirely to a religious life, building many temples and pagodas, and leaving all affairs of state in the hands of his four brothers. They ruled jointly, sitting together as a Council of State. This is thought to have been the origin of the Hlutdaw, the highest governing body under the king in the days of Burma's last royal house, the Konbaungset Dynasty (1752-1885). But, as very little is known of the earlier history of this institution or of the organization of the Pagan monarchy, the suggestion probably represents little more than the guesswork of later chroniclers.

With Htilominlo's reign the great age of temple-building comes to an end. He completed the majestic Gawdawpalin, which his father had founded, and built the Mahabodi, a copy of the Buddhagaya Temple, and the Htilominlo, named after himself. They were the last to be built in the grand style. Under his pious patronage monastic life flourished. The influence of Ceylon stimulated the production of several Pali treatises and commentaries, notably a law-book, the Dhammavilasa *dhammathat*, by a Mon monk of Dalla, which survives only in quotations in later works.

Htilominlo's son, Kyaswa (1234–50), emulated his father's piety and left the direction of the kingdom to his son Uzana. The latter reigned only four years after his father's death: he was accidentally killed in 1254 while hunting elephants. His son, Narathihapate (1254–87) witnessed the collapse of the monarchy. He was the typical eastern despot of fiction, without any of the redeeming features of his predecessors. He showed no zeal for religion, and his arbitrary and brutal behaviour caused his vassals to revolt. The pompous hyperbole of the inscription with which he dedicated the Mingalazedi Pagoda, stands out in sharp contrast to the genuine devotion and literary refinement which characterize those of his predecessors. In it he is styled "the supreme commander of a vast army of thirty-six million soldiers, the swallower of three hundred dishes of curry daily".

But he was not wholly responsible for the downfall of his kingdom. He lived at a time when external forces were gathering which were beyond the power of the Pagan monarchy to withstand. And there can be no doubt that the expenditure of so much energy in the founding of temples and monasteries had exhausted the country by the middle of the thirteenth century. The Mingalazedi Pagoda indeed gave rise to the Burmese proverb, 'the pagoda is finished and the great country ruined'. The kingdom itself had little cohesive force, when put to the test. It was a loose collection of districts run by feudal lords over whom the central government might have little control. And the

Mons of the south still cherished the memory of their lost independence.

With two centuries of continuous existence to its credit—a long period for an eastern monarchy—and associated with the prestige of a truly magnificent capital city, the Pagan dynasty might still have recovered its position and held its empire together, had it not been for the simultaneous onslaught of two foreign foes, the Tartars and the Shans. Against one or the other it might have survived, since Kublai Khan had too many irons in the fire to attempt the serious conquest of distant Burma; and without the debilitating effects of the Tartar invasions Pagan could have stood up successfully to the Shans. But the two series of attacks were almost interwoven, and the kingdom fell never to rise again.

The thirteenth century, which saw the culmination of Mediaeval Christendom in Europe, witnessed even more important events farther east. It was the period when Jenghis Khan and his successors founded the vast Mongol Empire stretching from the Caspian to the China Sea. Western Christendom, threatened by Ogdai Khan, the successor of Jenghis, was saved only by his death in 1242 after conquering Russia and ravaging Poland. Kublai Khan concentrated his attention on eastern Asia. In 1253 he annexed Yunnan. Then, having established himself as Emperor of China, he sent missions far and wide to demand the allegiance of all states which were traditionally regarded by the Middle Kingdom as its satellites. In 1271 his viceroy in Yunnan was instructed to claim from Pagan the tribute which had been paid by Narathihapate's predecessors. Had the king been willing to send a suitable acknowledgement of submission, he would in all probability have been left alone in peace. Instead, however, he refused even to receive the Chinese envoys.

Two years later the demand was renewed. It was conveyed by an embassy headed by the First Secretary of the Board of Rites, who was the bearer of a letter from Kublai Khan threatening war if the Burmese king refused to fulfil his duties 'towards the All-Highest'. Against the advice of his ministers Narathihapate seized the ambassador, his colleagues and their whole retinue, and put them all to death. When no immediate step was taken by the Chinese to avenge this insult, the rash king followed up his act of defiance by invading the state of Kaungai, on the Taping between Bhamo and Momein (Tengyueh), because its chief had submitted to the Mongols. The chief asked aid of Kublai Khan, who ordered the local garrisons to deal with the invaders. Thereupon a small Tartar force under the Governor of Tali repulsed the Burmese in an engagement known to Burmese history as the battle of Ngasaunggyan (1277) and graphically reported by the Venetian Marco Polo, who as a member of the Imperial Staff must have pieced the story together from the accounts of officers taking part in the action. Later in the same year a second Tartar force under the provincial governor Nasr-uddin followed up this victory by an advance into the Bhamo district. The Burmese retreated before him, but the excessive heat so distressed the Tartars that they retired without fighting any large-scale engagement.

The Burmese continued to raid the Yunnan frontier, and again in 1283 the Chinese invaded, heavily defeated them at Kaungsin and penetrated the Irrawaddy valley. There they contented themselves with planting garrisons; they did not attempt an advance on Pagan itself. Narathihapate, however, was panic-stricken. Firmly convinced that the Chinese would pursue their advance right up to his capital, he fled precipitately to Bassein in the Delta. With his departure all central authority vanished, northern Arakan proclaimed its independence and the Mons broke into open revolt.

From Bassein Narathihapate sent an envoy to Yunnan offering his humble submission, and it was accepted. But his prestige was irreparably damaged. In the eyes of his people he was Tarokpyemin, 'the king who ran away from the Chinese', and as such he has been known ever since in Burmese history. When he returned to Prome, hoping to collect an army and mend his shattered fortunes, his son Thihathu, its governor, put him to death (1287).

The country was now in such disorder that Kublai Khan's grandson, Prince Ye-su Timur, who was in Yunnan, decided that the opportunity to quench the independence of the proud kingdom was too good to be missed. At the head of a considerable army he fought his way down the Irrawaddy, occupied Pagan and sent out detachments far and wide to enforce submission. Actually the Chinese did not envisage the permanent occupation of the kingdom. The campaign of 1287 had been a costly one and the victors were now willing to reinstate the royal family in their capital city. Hence, when one of the sons of the Tarokpyemin, Kyawswa, the survivor of a bloodbath in the south, in which five of his brothers had perished, made his way to Pagan and submitted to the Chinese, they accorded him official recognition as its ruler. The kingdom, however, was no more. At Pegu a Mon leader, Tarabya, in league with Wareru, a Shan adventurer from Sukhotai in northern Siam, had eliminated Burmese rule south of Prome and Toungoo. In the north three Shan chiefs had gained control over the vital Kyauksè area and Pagan was a capital without a kingdom.

CHAPTER III

THE SHAN PENETRATION

THE Shans, the Laos and the Siamese of today are all descended from a racial group, cognate to the Chinese, and known among themselves as the T'ai. From the sixth century B.C. onwards Chinese records make frequent reference to these 'barbarians' south of the Yang-tse-Kiang. Early in the Christian era the T'ai came under Chinese suzerainty, but they were often in rebellion and ever anxious to assert their independence. In the middle of the seventh century they formed the powerful kingdom of Nanchao, which, as we have seen, exerted a far from inconsiderable influence upon the course of Burmese history before the rise of Pagan. T'ai tribes also found their way into south-eastern China on the one side and the Northern Shan States of Burma on the other. In 1229 T'ai immigrants founded the Ahom kingdom of Assam in the Bramaputra valley.

When in 1253 Kublai Khan conquered Nanchao, a spate of emigration ensued. Two T'ai chiefs defeated the Cambodians and established themselves at Sukhotai. It was from this place that Wareru in 1281 seized Martaban and proceeded to make himself master of Lower Burma. From northern Siam also the T'ai pressed gradually southwards into the Menam valley until finally they founded their most important state with its capital at Ayuthia.

The record of their penetration into Upper Burma is obscure, and modern writers of Burmese history have perhaps tended to exaggerate its extent. A Shan colony existed at Myinsaing before 1260. It was the practice of the Pagan kings to reward soldiers by gifts of irrigated land, and the colonists may have been a mercenary force serving in the Burmese army. A Shan chieftain from the hills took refuge there in 1260. His three sons were apparently educated at the court of Narathihapate. When Kyawswa succeeded his father at Pagan, he granted formal investiture to them of the principalities which they had acquired in the Kyauksè district during the Chinese invasions. Athinhkaya, the eldest, became prince of Myinsaing, Yazathinkyan, the second, chief of Mekkaya, and Thihathu, the youngest, chief of Pinle.

The Three Brothers soon threw off their allegiance to their suzerain. Finding his position intolerable because of their stranglehold on his food supplies, Kyawswa tried to call in external aid; whereupon they promptly seized and murdered him, and sacked and burnt the city of Pagan (1299). In the sack all its Chinese inhabitants were put to the sword. As a result the Yunnan government in 1300 despatched a punitive expedition against the Three Shan Brothers. Their resistance, however, was stubborn, and in the end the Chinese were persuaded to call off the attack on receipt of a considerable bribe. The Yunnan authorities, dissatisfied with the conduct of the campaign, executed all the leaders on their return, but sent no further expedition. Experience seems to have taught them that campaigns in Burma were expensive luxuries.

Pagan now drops completely out of the picture. The Chinese sack in 1287 had been terrible, but the Shan destruction in 1299 was decisive. Kyawswa's son Sawhnit was permitted to succeed him and ruled until his death in 1325, when he was followed by his son Uzana (1325-69), the last of the Anawrahta dynasty. But both were no more than petty chieftains. The real power was in the hands of the Three Shan Brothers and their successors. Myinsaing, however, was unfavourably sited to supplant Pagan as the capital of a kingdom: it was too far away from the Irrawaddy. Ava was the obvious site, but the Brahmins, who acted as the court soothsayers, declared against it. So in 1312 Thihathu, the sole survivor of the Three Brothers, planted his capital at Pinya, close by. Three years later one of his sons set up a separate state with its capital at Sagaing.

There was now no peace in the land; revolts and disorder prevailed to such an extent that men began to look back regretfully to the past as a golden age. An inscription of 1343 refers to Pagan as the 'fairest and dearest of lands'. The quarrels of Shan rulers inside Burma attracted further inroads of Shans from without, with the result that hundreds of Burmese refugees began to flee southwards to Toungoo on the Sittang river, where in 1280 a village had been fortified on a hill-spur (*taunggnu*) as a protection against slave raids from the neighbouring state of Karenni. In this way a new centre of Burmese power gradually came into existence, a stronghold against Shan domination, a nucleus from which in the course of time a new kingdom of Burma was to arise.

The separate states of Pinya and Sagaing lasted only until 1364. They were extinguished by a Shan chieftain, Thadomin-bya, descended from the founder of Sagaing on his mother's side. He then selected Ava at the confluence of the Myitngè and the Irrawaddy as the site of his capital. There he built a royal city on the traditional pattern followed by all Burmese capitals, calling it by the classical Pali name Ratanapura, 'city of gems'. He strove to conciliate Burmese national sentiment by claiming descent from the legendary kings of Tagaung.

The southern region of his kingdom, largely unaffected by Shan inroads, was in revolt, and his first task was to restore authority. While campaigning at Sagu, however, he died of small-pox at the early age of twenty-five (1368). It is significant that his successor, Mingyi Swasawke (1368–1401), who came to the throne through a palace intrigue, deemed it politic to claim descent from the Pagan royal house. Shan rulers, raiders, auxiliaries and colonists did indeed play a decisive role in the politics of Upper Burma, but the indications all go to show that Ava was essentially a Burmese city and the capital of a Burmese state. In time it won a prestige among the Burmese people such as Toungoo could never enjoy, so that while the 'Kingdom of Pegu' became a name for the Mon state in the south, the 'Kingdom of Ava' signified Burma proper, the land of the Burmese.

Ava too adopted the traditional Burmese policy of attempting to subjugate the Mons. Mingyi Swasawke aimed at controlling the Irrawaddy waterway down to the sea. Within a few years he had made good his authority as far south as Prome, which he conquered. Then in 1385 he challenged the independence of the Mon kingdom ruled by Razadarit of Pegu, and a long tussle ensued, which lasted far beyond his own reign. Year after year Burmese and Shan forces tried to fight their way down the Irrawaddy and the Sittang, for Toungoo also joined in the struggle.

It is difficult to estimate the part played by the Shans in this enterprise, or the extent to which they remained the dominating power in Ava itself. The Mon records mention contingents from the Shan states of the mountainous country beyond Burma proper. Sometimes they refer to the invaders simply as 'Shans'. But the fact remains that the Upper Burma inscriptions of this period are all composed in excellent Burmese, not in the Shan language, and that before the end of the 'Shan period' Ava witnessed the birth of Burmese vernacular literature. Hence the idea that these attacks upon the south may represent a war of Shan migration, as suggested by Harvey, must be discounted. Ava's wars with Pegu are an episode in the struggle for pre-dominance between the Burmese and the Mons, which begins in earnest with Anawrahta's conquest of Thaton, and is a principal factor in Burmese history till the end of the eighteenth century.

Minhkaung, who ruled energetically from 1401 to 1422, made great efforts to subdue Razadarit of Pegu and nearly succeeded. The Mons, however, widened the scope of the war by fomenting discord between Ava and the Shan States on the one side, and by obtaining the help of Arakan on the other. And when a Burmese army drove the king of Arakan to take refuge in Bengal, Razadarit sent an expedition up the Irrawaddy which penetrated as far as Sagaing before turning back. But Razadarit's position also was complicated by his own struggles with the Siamese states of Ayuthia, Kampengpet and Chiengmai. The tide of war therefore ebbed and flowed constantly. For a short time Burmese forces actually occupied some of the chief towns of the Delta, though in the end they were all cleared out and Mon authority restored. With the deaths of the rival kings, Minhkaung in 1422 and Razadarit in the following year, there was a temporary lull in the struggle.

The interference of Ava and Pegu in the affairs of Arakan had important consequences for that country. The Ava king placed his son-in-law on the throne of Arakan. The Mons in return invaded the country, killed the Burmese nominee and replaced him with a ruler chosen by Razadarit. In 1430, however, with the assistance of Bengal, the exiled king, Narameikhla, returned and was reinstated as the vassal of the Mohammedan

king of Gaur. He founded Mrohaung as his capital, and his
Mohammedan followers built a mosque there. From this time
onwards the Arakanese kings, although Buddhists, used
Mohammedan titles in addition to their own names. They
even issued medallions bearing the Kalima, the Mohammedan
confession of faith. The connection between Arakan and
India became even more pronounced when in 1459 an Arakanese king occupied Chittagong.

As the fifteenth century progressed, the rulers of Ava
became too much involved in dealing with their own unruly
vassals to spare energy for enterprises against the Mons. Shan
states such as Onbaung, Yawnghwe and Mohnyin up in the
mountains made common cause with rebellious Burmese local
lords and the land was in a chronic state of unrest. The interference of the Shan sawbwas reached its peak in the first half of
the sixteenth century, when Ava was fatally weakened by the
cession of the Kyaukse region to Toungoo. As Harvey puts it,
Upper Burma became 'a bedlam of snarling Shan states'. The
last four rulers of Ava, before its absorption into the reunited
kingdom of Burma in 1555, were all Shan sawbwas.

The one bright spot in all this welter of barbarism is the rise
of Burmese vernacular literature. As might be expected, it was
the product of monastic schools in whose calm seclusion the
culture of Pagan was guarded and cherished. That culture,
however, had its roots in the study of Pali literature. Hence the
fact that during a period of Shan dominance the national
literature had its birth is an illustration of the strength of
Burmese nationalism not without significance. Much of it is
poetry and consists of translations or paraphrases of sacred
stories such as Shin Aggathamahdi's versions of the *jataka*
stories of the Buddha, composed early in the sixteenth century.
But the period also produced Shin Thilawuntha's Yazawingyaw
chronicle, the earliest Burmese history extant. The compiler
was a monk of Taungdwingyi in Magwe district. Expelled for
writing poetry which his abbot considered profane, he made his
way to Ava, where King Minhkaung II built him a monastery
named Yatanabiman. There he wrote his chronicle, some more
poems still treasured today, and a grammatical treatise. His life
covered the period 1453-1520. Unfortunately his chronicle had

little bearing on the events of his own day: it is a largely valueless collection of mythical tales. Of the same period is the monkish poet Shin Uttamagyaw, whose well-known poem *Tawla* still survives. Dating probably from this period also is a collection of *angyin* verse on the fifty-five styles of hairdressing used by maids-of-honour at the Court of Ava. The writer herself was a maid-of-honour named Yaweshinhtwe.

CHAPTER IV

THE MON HEGEMONY

WARERU, who seized Martaban in 1281, is said to have been a Shan pedlar born at Donwun in Thaton district. He took service with the ruler of Sukhotai, became Captain of the Guard, eloped with his chief's daughter and ran away to seek his fortune in Burma. After gaining possession of Martaban, he joined hands with Tarabya of Pegu in expelling the Burmese governors from the Mon country. In 1287, when they had successfully completed their task, Tarabya tried to seize Wareru, but failed and was murdered by his colleague. Wareru thereupon obtained the recognition of China as the ruler of Lower Burma and founded a kingdom which lasted until 1539. Martaban was its first capital, and remained so until 1369. It stretched southwards as far as Tenasserim for a time; but there were constant boundary disputes with Siam, which ultimately secured all the territory south of Tavoy.

Wareru's chief monument today is the *dhammathat* which bears his name and is the earliest law-book in Burma still extant. It consists of laws ascribed to the ancient Indian sage, Manu, and brought to Burma by Hindu colonists. The collection was made at Wareru's command, by monks from the writings of earlier Mon scholars preserved in the monasteries of his kingdom.

When the kingdom of Ayuthia was founded in 1350, the Siamese claimed the Mon provinces of Tenasserim, Moulmein and Martaban. A Siamese raid in 1363 forced the Mon king to abandon Martaban, and for a short time the capital was established at Donwun, Wareru's birthplace. In 1369, however, Binnya U (1353–85) set up his palace at Pegu, which from this time onwards became the Mon capital. His successor, Razadarit (1385–1423), as we have seen in the previous chapter, defended his realm successfully against repeated attacks by the Burmese and the Shans. He was an able administrator, who maintained law and order with a firm hand. According to

Burmese tradition, he organized the kingdom into thirty-two provinces.

After his death the Mons enjoyed a long period of peace and prosperity. Many foreign traders were attracted to the capital, which became well-known to the outside world as a centre of commerce. As such it is mentioned by the Russian merchant, Nitikin, who travelled in the East about 1470. Its fifteenth-century rulers were, like those of old Pagan, chiefly interested in the development of religion. Missions were sent to Ceylon and on their return stimulated an important religious revival, which affected the whole of Burma. Its centre was the Kalyani *thein* near Pegu, so named because its original monks had been ordained on the banks of the Kalyani river in Ceylon. Kalyani ordination became the standard form for the whole country. The story of the reforms is told in the Kalyani inscriptions erected by King Dammazedi (1472–92).

Dammazedi was the greatest of the rulers of Wareru's line. His reign was a time of peace and he himself was a mild ruler, famous for his wisdom. A collection of his rulings, the Dammazedi *pyatton*, is still extant. He maintained friendly intercourse with Yunnan and revived the practice of sending missions to Buddhagaya. He was a Buddhist ruler of the best type, deeply solicitous for the purification of religion. Under him civilization flourished, and the condition of the Mon country stands out in sharp contrast with the disorder and savagery which characterized the Ava kingdom. When he died he was honoured as a saint and a pagoda was erected over his bones.

The Mon kingdom possessed two great pagodas of especial sanctity, the Shwemawdaw at Pegu and the Shwe Dagon at the small stockaded fishing-town of Dagon, now Rangoon, the capital of modern Burma. The early history of both the town and its pagoda is legendary. According to the Mahayazawin the latter was founded in the lifetime of Gautama, and was erected over eight hairs of his head. Modern historical scholarship knows nothing of the town before the fourteenth century. Its earliest historical name is the Mon word *Dagun*. The importance of the town grew with that of the pagoda. Originally only twenty-seven feet high, it was raised to a height of sixty-six feet in 1362 by King Binnya U as an act of special piety. Dammazedi's immediate predecessor, his mother-in-law Queen Shinsawbu (1453–72), raised its height to 129 feet. She terraced the hill on which it stands, paved the top terrace with flagstones, and assigned land and hereditary slaves for its maintenance. When in 1472 she yielded up the throne to Dammazedi, she retired to Dagon, and during her last illness had her bed placed so that she could rest her dying eyes upon the gilded dome of the sacred fane. The Mon face of the Shwe Dagon inscription catalogues a list of repairs beginning in 1436 and finishing during Dammazedi's reign. It mentions Queen Shinsawbu under a terrific Pali name of sixty-six letters. By the beginning of the sixteenth century the pagoda had become the most famous place of pilgrimage in Burma.

The town of Dagon itself, however, was still comparatively insignificant. Its value as a port does not seem to have been realized until the middle of the eighteenth century. The chief Mon ports were Syriam, just below Dagon, Bassein in the Delta, Martaban and Pegu itself. It was to these that the earliest recorded visitors to Burma came in the fifteenth century. The first was a Venetian merchant of noble family, Nicolo di Conti, who toured India and parts of south-east Asia somewhere between 1420 and 1444. He came to Arakan in 1435, travelled overland to Ava, which he described as a noble city fifteen miles in circumference, and stayed four months in Pegu. In Ava he saw the royal white elephant, which, he said, was dust-coloured with unsightly skewbald patches.

In 1496 Pegu was visited by another Italian, the Genoese Hieronomo de Santo Stefano. He brought with him a valuable stock of merchandise, which he disposed of to King Binnya Ran, who kept him waiting eighteen months for payment. To Binnya Ran's court at Pegu came yet another Italian merchant, Ludovico di Varthema, who was vastly impressed by its magnificence. The king, he wrote, wore more rubies than the value of a very large city, while Pegu abounded with 'good houses and palaces built of stone with lime'. The country possessed valuable forests with abundant elephants. A rich trade was carried on in shellac, sandal-wood, brazil-wood, cotton, silk and rubies, and was the main source of the royal

revenue. Neither Santo Stefano nor Varthema was able to
visit Ava: conditions beyond the confines of the Mon kingdom
were too anarchic.

But the days of the Mon Kingdom itself with its gracious
civilization were now drawing to a close. Binnya Ran's successor,
Takayutpi (1526–39), was the last of his house. A new age was
dawning, with a Burmese national movement of expansion
gathering force in the north, and the conquest of Malacca in
1511 by the Portuguese Don Affonso de Albuquerque. With
the latter the Mons concluded a commercial agreement under
which Portuguese merchants might come to trade at Martaban
and Pegu. When some years later the Burmese leader Tabinshwehti invaded the Mon country and dethroned Takayutpi,
Portuguese adventurers flocked to the country to take service in
his armies and Burma began to learn the use of firearms.

CHAPTER V

THE RISE OF THE TOUNGOO DYNASTY

THE valley of the Sittang lay away from the direct route between Ava and the Delta and the settlement, which grew up around Toungoo, was therefore in a happier position than Prome on the Irrawaddy in the same latitude. In this way its early development as a haven of refuge for Burmese escaping from Shan rule was almost unhampered. Nominally it owed allegiance to Pagan, but by the middle of the fourteenth century its strength was such that its chief, Thinhkaba (1347–58), assumed the royal title and built himself a palace. During the reign of his son Pyanchi (1358–77) the liquidation of Sagaing and Pinya brought a fresh wave of Burmese immigrants to Toungoo. In an inscription, which he set up at Pagan to record a visit paid there for the purpose of making offerings at its shrines, Pyanchi mentions the fact that he and his wife had welcomed refugees from the Shan terror.

In the long wars between Ava and Pegu the Toungoo rulers were sometimes ranged with Ava in its onslaught upon the Mons. From time to time also attempts were made by both Ava and Pegu to quench the independence of Toungoo. The little state led a chequered existence: it had no regular succession of rulers and no ruling family maintained its power for long. The turning-point in its history came with the reign of Minkyinyo (1486–1531). Profiting by the chaos and weakness then reigning in the Ava kingdom, he acquired large additions to his territory, including the Kyauksè irrigation area. In 1527, when the Shans reoccupied Ava, so many Burmese chiefs fled to take service with him, that he became the most powerful ruler in Burma. He was in the middle of preparations for the conquest of Pegu, when he died in 1531, and it fell to his son and successor, Tabinshwehti (1531–1550), to carry this project to success.

Tabinshwehti started his reign with a gesture of sublime audacity. He determined to carry out the ear-boring ceremony at the Shwemawdaw Pagoda at Pegu, and with a chosen band of armed followers did so under the very nose of King Takayutpi. Four years later he began the systematic conquest of the Mon kingdom. At first sight it would seem a perilous policy to launch a big campaign in the south before strengthening his position against the Shans in the north. But they possessed no leader of eminence, and he probably gambled on their congenital incapacity for combined action. The deciding factor may have been the riches of Pegu.

The Delta was easily conquered. Bassein and Myaungmya fell in the first campaign. Pegu itself, however, was a far more difficult proposition. For four years it resisted every attack, and was only finally taken by stratagem in 1539. King Takayutpi fled to Prome closely pursued by Tabinshwehti and his brilliant comrade-in-arms and brother-in-law, Bayinnaung. The attack on Prome miscarried. The Shan ruler of Ava came downstream with a large flotilla to relieve it, and the Burmese forces had to retreat. Tabinshwehti's position, however, was eased by the death of Takayutpi. A large proportion of the Mon chiefs came to offer their allegiance and were well received. It was the conqueror's policy to respect Mon customs and institutions, and he used all the arts of conciliation. He was no mere warrior leader.

Foiled before Prome, he next turned his attention to the port of Martaban. For the attack he recruited Mon levies and a force of Portuguese mercenaries armed with muskets and light artillery. Martaban also was defended by a company of Portuguese, but they deserted and Tabinshwehti carried the city by storm. For three days massacre and looting raged and the booty was immense. It was a dreadful act of savagery, which cannot be reconciled with his general policy of winning over the Mons; but with an army swelled with mercenaries it was inevitable. And it frightened the rest of the Mons into submission. Moulmein surrendered without a blow, and the remainder of the Mon territory as far as the Siamese frontier at Tavoy fell into Burmese hands. Tabinshwehti attoned for his cruelty by placing new spires on Mon pagodas and making costly offerings at the Shwe Dagon.

Martaban fell in 1541. In the following year the attack on Prome was renewed. Vain attempts were made by both Arakan

and Ava to relieve it. After a five months' siege it was starved
into submission and treated to the same punishment as Martaban. Its capture opened the way to central Burma up the Irrawaddy waterway. This threat caused the squabbling Shan
sawbwas of the north to make common cause. In 1544 the
ruler of Ava, Hkonmaing, and the sawbwas of six states,
Mohnyin, Momeik, Hsenwi, Bhamo, Yawnghwe and Monè,
united in a counter-attack to recover Prome. Their flotilla of
war-boats was easily dispersed by Tabinshwehti's Portuguese
gunners and a decisive victory resulted. Following it up with all
speed, Tabinshwehti occupied all the country up to the north of
Minbu and Myingyan districts. He was crowned king of Burma
at the ruined city of Pagan. Then, as if he feared this last act
might be misunderstood by his Mon subjects, he staged a
further coronation ceremony at Pegu, in which both Mon and
Burmese rites were used (1546). He made no attempt to carry
his conquests farther north by an attack upon Ava. Pegu, not
Pagan or Toungoo, was his capital, and his main efforts at
consolidation were confined to the south and centre.

   Consolidation is perhaps hardly an appropriate description
of his policy, if it is taken to imply concentration upon reorganization and administration; for his warlike activities continued
without respite. His next attacks were delivered against Arakan
and Siam. The Arakanese had joined with the Shans in attempting to break up his second siege of Prome, and Siam threatened
Tavoy. Both invasions failed after much initial success. The
defences of Mrohaung, the capital of Arakan, were too strong
for him, and the expedition had to be called off (1546–47). In
the same way the Siam invasion of 1547–48 penetrated right up
to Ayuthia, but the Siamese artillery, manned by Portuguese,
defied all the efforts of the besiegers. This was the first of a
series of Burmese attempts to subjugate Siam. Both Burmese
and Siamese chronicles assign to it a cause which in European
eyes has appeared frivolous, namely the refusal of the king of
Siam to surrender his white elephants to Tabinshwehti. But
Tabinshwehti's policy must be interpreted in the light of the
Shan threat to Burma. His conquest of the Mon kingdom had
been the first move in the bigger game of uniting Burma against
the Shans. It was only natural therefore that, as soon as he felt

strong enough, he should seek to paralyse the most powerful and best organized of all the Shan states, and one which cherished claims to much of the territory he had conquered from the Mons.

The white elephant, however, was a symbol which counted for much in the eyes of a Buddhist ruler, not to mention his people. The Buddhist kings of Indo-China had borrowed from Hinduism much of their court ceremonial. In Burma, Siam, Cambodia and Champa, and in a host of smaller states, Brahman astrologers and soothsayers were masters of the ceremonies. As interpreters of the omens and repositories of ancient tradition their influence was great. One Hindu tradition in particular, that of a legendary Chakravartin or Universal Monarch, caused every ambitious ruler to dream dreams of world dominion. But not world dominion in the vulgar sense: he aspired to become a Buddhist Saviour, a Maitreya, who would extend the blessings of the Law to the whole world, and restore the Golden Age. For such a destiny the possession of a white elephant was essential, for had not the Buddha in one of his previous incarnations been a white elephant? Every Buddhist ruler therefore strove to acquire such an animal, and at this period with all the greater zest, since India, the source of the tradition, had come under Mohammedan domination.

After the failure of his Siam expedition Tabinshwehti, though still a young man, lost his morale. Under the influence of a disreputable Portuguese favourite he became a confirmed drunkard, and his kingdom began to fall apart. His brother-in-law, Bayinnaung, took control as regent, but soon found himself in a desperate plight. The Mons rebelled, murdered Tabinshwehti (1550), and a claimant of the old royal family seized the throne of Pegu. The governors of Prome and Toungoo proclaimed their independence. The old days of warring kinglets seemed about to return.

But to a born leader of men, and Bayinnaung was the greatest ever produced by Burma, the situation was by no means hopeless. The allegiance of the Mons was divided between two rival leaders, each bidding for the throne. And there were many people, both Burmese and Mons, who preferred the security of a single united kingdom to the chaos which threatened. There was also Burmese national sentiment, which had been the foundation of the success of Minkyinyo and Tabinshwehti, and to which Bayinnaung now turned in his extremity. With the help of a Portuguese mercenary leader, Diogo Soarez de Mello, he fell upon Toungoo, took it, and was crowned there as Tabinshwehti's successor. From thence he carried out a lightning campaign, reducing central Burma, Prome and finally Pegu, which he treated to a frightful punishment. With its capture the Mon revolt collapsed. Before the end of 1551 his sway was acknowledged throughout the length and breadth of Tabinshwehti's realm. Smim Htaw, the defender of Pegu, the 'Xemindo' of the fourth book of the great De Barros-Couto history, which tells the story of these campaigns with much picturesque detail, was hunted to his death in the hills around Sittaung. He was the last of Wareru's line.

Bayinnaung's task was still only half completed. His life was indeed, as Harvey puts it, "the greatest explosion of human energy ever seen in Burma". Four years after the re-establishment of his rule in Pegu he began to develop his great counterattack upon the Shan States, which had lasting effects upon his country's history. It opened with the conquest of Ava in 1555, followed immediately by the subjugation of the north as far as Bangyi in Monyua district and Myedu in Shwebo district. Succeeding years up to 1562 saw campaigns against Manipur and the Shan states of Bhamo, Chiengmai and Linzin, and raids up the Taping and Shweli rivers in the direction of Yunnan. It was not all plain sailing: the tide of success ebbed and flowed. There were chronic revolts necessitating further campaigns, which ended in mass deportations and the exaction of heavy tribute. In the end, however, most of the Shan states on the fringe of Burma were forced to accept his suzerainty, and it is from these campaigns that the Burmese overlordship of modern times dates. The deportations brought crowds of skilled craftsmen into Burma, and it is thought that the finer sort of Burmese lacquerware, called *yun*, was introduced during this period by deported artisans belonging to the Yun or Laos Shan tribes of the Chiengmai region.

The reduction of the Shan states in the north-east naturally led on to the resumption of the struggle with Siam. It began in

1563, and the *casus belli* was again the White Elephant question. King Chakrap'at of Ayuthia possessed four according to the Burmese account. Bayinnaung asked for one and his request was refused. The Siamese give a slightly different version of the number, but in general the two accounts supplement each other, and from them a reasonably authentic picture may be pieced together of the exhausting struggle, which went on between the two states for the rest of the century and beyond.

Bayinnaung's first campaign succeeded beyond all expectations. Ayuthia surrendered, and the conqueror brought back to Pegu a captive king, princes as hostages, a princess to grace his harem and four white elephants. The amount of loot was prodigious. A Siamese prince was placed on the throne as vassal ruler supported by a Burmese army of occupation. So sudden a collapse, however, was more apparent than real. The kingdom as a whole was not systematically reduced to obedience, and as soon as Bayinnaung's back was turned, rebellion flared up. It was headed by the Raja of Patani, while in the north the rulers of Chiengmai and Linzin (Viengchang) rose against the Burmese. So a second time Bayinnaung led his forces into Siam and carried out a repeat performance of the first expedition. Ayuthia was again captured, and another puppet ruler placed upon its throne. Chiengmai had to surrender its king, who was brought to Pegu as a hostage. Linzin could not be held down, and there was constant fighting during the rest of Bayinnaung's life.

But Ayuthia gave him no further trouble. Nevertheless his weakness lay in his failure to develop effective control over his wide dominions. Each district was under feudal lords, whose loyalty was ever uncertain. Only the outstanding personality of the great leader held together the loosely-knit empire, and during this absence on a distant campaign rebellions broke out only too easily. After his first conquest of Ayuthia he was forced to hurry home because the Mons of the Pegu area made common cause with Shan and Siamese deportees in an attack upon the city and burnt it to the ground. But while he lived he sternly repressed all opposition, and his authority so impressed the Venetian prospector, Caesar Frederick, who visited Pegu in

1569, that he wrote: "He far exceeds the power of the Great Turk in treasure and strength."

According to Burmese ideas he was a model Buddhist king. He made costly offerings at the great pagodas, founded monasteries, distributed copies of the scriptures, fed monks, supervised mass ordinations at the Kalyani *thein*, and assembled famous scholars to compile and prescribe law books. To demonstrate his devotion to the doctrine of *ahimsa* he forbade all animal sacrifices, including such famous observances as the Mohammedan Bakrid festival, Shan funeral sacrifices and the slaughter of white animals to the Mahagiri Nat at Mount Popa. His repair of the Shwe Dagon Pagoda after the earthquake of 1564 was one of the most notable in its history, for he raised its height considerably and added a new spire.

His chief religious foundation was the Mahazedi Pagoda at Pegu. Among other relics it enshrined a tooth of Buddha presented by the Raja of Colombo in Ceylon. The events leading up to the presentation of this much-prized relic form one of the most striking incidents in the history of Portuguese Asia. In 1560 the Viceroy of Goa, Dom Constantino de Bragança, hearing that some of the converts made by St. Francis Xavier in Ceylon were being persecuted by the Raja of Jafna, a state on the north coast, led a punitive expedition, which took and sacked the city of Jafna. Among the loot was a tooth set in gold in a jewelled casket. Report had it that this was the Kandy Tooth, one of the most famous of Buddhist relics, which had been temporarily loaned to Jafna by the king of Kandy. It was not long before the startling news reached Bayinnaung that the Tooth had been captured by the Portuguese and taken to Goa. Since his accession he had on several occasions made offerings to it; he had provided for lights to burn at its shrine in the Temple of Kandy, and had sent craftsmen to beautify the building. He had even sent a broom for use there made from his own and his chief queen's hair. He now despatched envoys to the Viceroy offering a princely sum of money for the purchase of the relic. He confidently believed that with the White Elephant of Siam and the Tooth of Kandy in his possession he would be the greatest monarch in the world.

The Viceroy was only too willing to accept the offer. The

Portuguese officers, who were to take it to Pegu, planned to make fortunes for themselves by exhibiting the Tooth at various places on the way to Burma. But the Archbishop of Goa insisted upon the matter being referred to the Inquisition, and the Viceroy dared not refuse. After profound discussion the Holy Office resolved that so dangerous an idol must be destroyed. The sentence was solemnly carried out in the presence of a huge crowd, among whom as horrified spectators were the Burmese envoys. The Archbishop ground the Tooth to powder in a large mortar with a heavy pestle. It was then burnt and the ashes consigned to the sea (1561).

Thirteen years later Bayinnaung sent envoys to Colombo to request the hand of a princess in marriage. As a wedding present the Raja sent with the princess a tooth, which he swore was the real Kandy relic. It had been hidden by the Raja of Jafna, when the Portuguese entered his city, and a monkey's tooth palmed off on the Viceroy. How the true relic came into the hands of the Raja of Colombo was never explained. In 1576 the princess and the tooth arrived in Burma and were given a reception of the utmost magnificence, after which, in a casket of gold, studded with rubies and emeralds, the tooth was deposited in the relic chamber beneath the Mahazedi Pagoda. It was useless for the king of Kandy to announce that the real Tooth had never been in the hands of either the Raja of Jafna, the Portuguese or the Raja of Colombo, since it had never left its Temple at Kandy. It was equally useless for him to protest to Bayinnaung that even the princess was spurious, since the Raja of Colombo had no daughter.

After the destruction of Pegu by the rebels in 1564, Bayinnaung rebuilt the city on a far grander scale, furnishing it with twenty gates, each named after the vassal responsible for its construction. Pegu became once more a great centre of commerce, the resort of merchants from many distant lands. Spaciously laid out with wide streets planted with shady trees, it was an impressive sight to European visitors. Here is Caesar Frederick's description of it as it was in 1569:

"In the new Citie is the Palace of the King and his abiding place with all his Barons and nobles and gentlemen

... it is a great citie, very plaine and flat, and foure square, walled round about, and with ditches which compass the wall about with Water, in which Ditches are many Crocodiles. It hath no Draw-bridges, yet it hath twenty Gates five for every square in the Walls ... Within the gate there is a faire large Court, from one side to the other, wherein there are made places for the strongest and stoutest Elephants, he hath foure that be white, a thing so rare, that a man shall hardly finde another King that hath any such, as if this King know any other that hath white Elephants, he sendeth for them as for a gift. The time that I was there, there were two brought out of a farre Countrie, and that cost me something the sight of them, for that they command the Merchants to goe to see them, and then they must give something to the men that bring them: the Brokers of the Merchants give for every man half a Ducket, which they call a *Tansa*, which amounteth to a great summe, for the number of Merchants that are in the Citie."

Like Tabinshwehti Bayinnaung treated the Mons with great respect. His commander-in-chief, Binnya Dala, and several of his principal officers of state were Mons. But for his incessant wars he might have drawn closer the bonds between Mons and Burmese. Unfortunately it was the Mons and their land that had to bear the chief burdens imposed by his extravagant policy. Famine reigned in the Delta in 1567 because through the drain on its manpower for service with the forces its rich lands could not be adequately cultivated. His Portuguese mercenaries tended to get out of hand, and preyed upon the land. On one occasion at Martaban, when they killed some of his personal messengers in a brawl, ninety of them marched through the town with colours flying, and defied arrest. War was his only answer to the problems of statecraft, and his wars impoverished his people.

Nandabayin, who succeeded to the throne in 1581, reaped the harvest sown by his father. Rebellions at once broke out. From Ava to Moulmein there was never a year without a rising somewhere. At first the new king was successful and repressed each one with ferocity. In 1583 the Venetian, Gasparo Balbi, was the horrified spectator of a mass execution of court grandees

and their families who were implicated in a revolt led by the
Viceroy of Ava. But he soon became involved in a new series of
struggles with Siam, which brought disaster to himself and his
country.

Siam's plight after its conquest by Bayinnaung was indeed
pitiable. The Burmese deported thousands of people as slaves.
Thousands more were carried away by Siam's old enemy,
Cambodia, which seized the opportunity to launch repeated
invasions. The Burmese left the vassal king, Maha T'ammaraja,
to cope with these as best he could, though at the same time
demanding a crippling tribute. With Nandabayin's accession,
however, Siam's hopes began to rise. Her brilliant young Crown
Prince, Naresuen, who was called upon by the new king to aid
him in putting down Burmese rebels, discovered that Burma
was no longer strong. On returning home he became the leader
of a party determined to throw off the Burmese yoke. When the
Ava Viceroy rebelled, Naresuen invaded Lower Burma and
threatened Pegu; but the return of the victorious Nandabayin
forced him to beat a hasty retreat. Nandabayin sent a pursuing
force, but Naresuen turned and defeated it on the banks of the
Sittaung river. Another Burmese force, sent to quell a Shan
revolt, was driven out of northern Siam by an army despatched
by Naresuen; and he followed up this success by defeating two
vassal chiefs, who had sided with the Burmese.

Nandabayin now decided that a full-scale invasion of Siam
was called for. He launched it late in the year 1584, and it was a
complete failure. It was the first of a series, all of them disastrous. The turning-point came in 1593 when his eldest son,
the Crown Prince, was defeated and killed by the Siamese.
Thenceforward it was the Siamese who came raiding and looting
into Burma: the initiative lay with them. Naresuen had
succeeded his father as king in 1590, and having achieved his
first objective, that of freeing his country from the Burmese,
was now seeking the recovery of the Mon provinces upon which
Siam had long-standing claims. In 1595 he appeared before the
walls of Pegu. He failed to take it, but seems to have annexed
Martaban and Tavoy.

From the beginning the full brunt of this exhausting struggle
had fallen on the hapless Mons. Not only was their land laid

waste, but they were branded and conscripted for forced labour
or military service. Thousands took refuge in the monasteries
and assumed the yellow robe in order to escape the appalling
hardships of the disastrous campaigns. But Nandabayin
ordered them to be unfrocked, and many were executed. Their
desperate rebellions were met with the most savage reprisals.
Hence it is not to be wondered at that, when Naresuen withdrew from Pegu in 1595, thousands of Mons fled with his army
into Siamese territory away from the Burmese terror. It was the
first of many periodic migrations, which went on at intervals up
to the nineteenth century. And as the tide of war flowed back-
wards and forwards, the Delta region, now one of the richest
agricultural districts in the world, became depopulated and
famine-stricken.

The climax came in 1599. With Toungoo, Chiengmai and
Prome in revolt, Nandabayin had to face another Siamese
invasion. But the knock-out blow was delivered from another
quarter: a powerful Arakanese fleet seized the port of Syriam and
joined with the rebel chief of Toungoo in besieging Pegu.
Nandabayin, unable to hold out against their combined forces,
surrendered to the Toungoo chief, who divided the plunder of
the city with the Arakanese and returned home, taking with
him the captive king and the Ceylon tooth from the Mahazedi
Pagoda. The Arakanese set fire to the city and made off with
their portion of the loot, including a daughter of Nandabayin
and a white elephant. In addition they deported some thousands
of Delta families.

The Siamese invading army arrived to find Pegu in ruins.
They therefore marched against Toungoo, but failed to take it.
They sustained so serious a defeat that Naresuen returned to
Ayuthia with only a remnant of his army. The united kingdom
of Burma and Pegu, however, was for the time being wrecked.
Nandabayin was murdered soon after his arrival at Toungoo.
Siam held its territory from Martaban southwards. A parcel of
warring chiefs divided the remainder of the country between
them, while Syriam, its chief port, was in the hands of a Portu-
guese adventurer, Felipe de Brito, nominally in the service of
Arakan, but ambitious to carve out a domain for himself in
Lower Burma.

CHAPTER VI

THE COMING OF THE EUROPEAN

BURMA was practically unknown to Europeans before the end
of the fourteenth century, when Marco Polo's book appeared
with its description of the war waged by Kublai Khan against
the 'King of Mien and Bangola'. The word 'Mien', as we have
seen above, was the Chinese word for Burma. 'Bangola' is Polo's
word for Bengal; but whether he confused Pegu with Bengal or
the king of Burma claimed that country as part of his empire is
uncertain. Whether Polo actually set foot on Burmese soil is
equally uncertain. As an imperial official he went to Yunnan
in connection with the Burma expeditions of 1282–84. But his
description of the capital city of Mien as a great and noble one
with two splendid towers, one of gold and one of silver, hung about
with bells which tinkled in the breeze, reads like mere hearsay.
On the other hand his account of the panic caused among the
king of Burma's elephants by the Tartar archers at the battle of
Ngasaunggyan (1277) is obviously authentic. His book also contains a few details of information concerning one of the semi-
independent Laos states on the fringe of Burma. There is
abundance of gold and elephants, he says, and many kinds of
spices. The people drink rice wine and tattoo their bodies with
figures of beasts and birds.

Thus was Burma introduced to the West; and although
Polo's description of the East was at first considered fantastic,
his geographical ideas were incorporated in the Catalan Map of
1375, which was apparently the first European map to include
Burma. Nicolo di Conti, who, as we have seen, came to Burma
in 1435, calls the country Machin, a corruption of Maha Chin
(Great China), the term applied in India to all lands east of the
Ganges.

Although after his conquest of Malacca in 1511 Albuquerque is said to have sent an embassy to the kingdom of Pegu,
regular trading relations did not result. This was probably
because the country lay away from the main trade routes to the

Spice Islands, while its commodities, exported through
Martaban, could be purchased at Malacca. And it was not until
much later that Europeans came to realize the value of its teak
forests. But if few traders appeared the number of Portuguese
adventurers, who took service in the fighting forces of Arakan,
Pegu and Siam, was considerable. Their skill with firearms was
their great asset. The danger was that they might be tempted to
play a decisive role in the political sphere. While the government was in the hands of a ruler of outstanding personality,
such a policy was out of the question; their numbers were too
few. But when at the end of the century Burma lay defeated and
divided, Felipe de Brito, who had seized Syriam for the king of
Arakan, decided that the moment was ripe for a game of far
higher stakes, and tried to enlist the support of Goa for his
plans. At almost the same time another Portuguese adventurer,
Sebastião Gonzales Tibao, with the active support of Goa,
attempted a similar role in Arakan, using Dianga close to
Chittagong as his base.

The Portuguese, however, came to the East not only to seek
their fortunes, but also to spread the Catholic religion and
crusade against Islam. In 1554 the first Catholic priests arrived
in Burma. They were two Dominican friars, Gaspar de Cruz
and Bomferrus, who came as chaplains to the seaport Portuguese. Bomferrus is said to have studied the Mon language.
But they were not well received by the *feringhi*, as the Portuguese freebooters were called in the East, and in 1557 they left,
declaring that they would rather preach among pigs like St.
Anthony. De Brito, on the other hand, took with him as chaplains to Syriam two Jesuits, Pimenta and Boves, who built a
church there, and after the recapture of the place by the
Burmese in 1613 accompanied the Portuguese captives up
country to the villages where they were settled by King
Anaukpetlun. Their accounts of the conditions of the country,
when they first arrived there in 1600, are included in Hakluyt's
great collection, and describe a scene of appalling devastation
and desolation.

Few of the Portuguese filibusters wrote accounts of Burma.
But one of them, the incomparable Ferdinand Mendes Pinto,
devoted no less than seven chapters of the story of his adven-

tures to the wars of Tabinshwehti and Bayinnaung. His extravagant claims led him to be dubbed a liar by seventeenth-century detractors, but modern scholars have found that the general picture he paints of Asia is authentic. The trouble is that in its details his *Peregrination* defies analysis by normal canons of criticism. Duarte Barbosa, writing at the end of the sixteenth century, included in his *Description of the Coasts of East Africa and Malabar* an account of Burma, which must have been compiled from materials supplied by *feringhi* who had served there. Though unreliable in many ways, it contains useful information about commerce. He shows that all the external trade of the country was in Mohammedan (i.e. Arab and Indian) hands. He mentions the export of rice to Malacca and Sumatra, the fine quality of Burmese lac and the huge Martaban jars, which were used on ships for the carriage of water and rice.

Caesar Frederick gives us easily the best account of six-teenth-century Burma. Thomas Hickock's translation of it was incorporated by Hakluyt in his *Principal Navigations* along with the narrative of Ralph Fitch, the first recorded Englishman to visit Burma. Caesar Frederick went there in 1569 and saw Bayin-naung in all his glory. Fitch was there twice, in 1587 and again in 1588, during the ill-fated reign of Nandabayin. On the outward journey Fitch and his companions had had the unpleasant experience of being arrested as spies at Goa. Hence he kept no diary of his travels for fear of having incriminating documents about him, should he encounter further trouble with the Portuguese. In writing his account for Hakluyt therefore he made extensive use of Caesar Frederick's. Much of his story indeed is little more than a boiled-down edition of the Venetian's. This is all the more unfortunate, since, when he has to rely upon his own memory, he has some interesting things to say.

Caesar Frederick wrote neither as a geographer nor as a traveller, but as a trading prospector. As a guide-book for intending traders it is unsurpassed. He describes the import of Indian textiles from the Coromandel Coast and Bengal through the ports of Pegu, Syriam and Bassein into Lower Burma, and the trade between those ports and Malacca, Sumatra and the Red

Sea. He describes also the strict examination of goods at the
ports by the customs officers, the methods in use for transporting
merchandise inland along the rivers and creeks, the brokerage
system by which all commercial transactions were conducted
and the general conditions affecting foreign merchants. He
devotes attention to the currency question. All payments, he
says, had to be made in a mixture of copper and lead called
ganza (Sanskrit *kansa*—bell metal), which was used by weight.
The standard amount was the Indian viss (3·65 lb. avoirdupois),
subdivided into 100 ticals. There was no coinage. To prevent
fraud 'by putting overmuch lead into them', it was necessary
to employ the services of one of the public assayers at the fixed
rate of two viss of *ganza* a month. "By this meanes," he says,
"the Merchant with the charges of two *Byzes* a moneth,
receiveth and payeth out his money without loss or trouble."
One viss of *ganza* was worth half a ducat of Venetian money.

His detailed description of Burma's imports, and the
sources from which they came, stands out in contrast with his
brief note on the subject of exports: "The Merchandizes that
go out of Pegu are Gold, Silver, Rubies, Saphires, Spinelles,
great store of Beniamin (benzoin), long Pepper, Lead, Lacca
(lac), Rice, Wine, some Sugar, yet there might be great store of
Sugar made in the Countrey, for they have abundance of Canes,
but they give them to Elephants to eate, and the people consume
great store of them for food, and many more do they consume in
vaine things."

He gives some very useful information regarding the effect
of the monsoon on sailings across the Bay from the Coromandel
Coast. The usual custom, he says, was for ships to leave the
Coast not later than the eleventh or twelfth of September. "For
in those parts the winds blowe firmly for certain times, with the
which they goe to Pegu with the wind in poope, and if they
arrive not there before the wind change, and get ground to
anchor perforce they must return back again: for that the gales
of the winde blowe there for three or foure moneths together
in one place with great force." Native shipping in those days
found it too dangerous to cross the Bay during the height of the
south-west monsoon; skippers had to time their sailings so as to
get across in the short period of comparative lull just before the

changeover to the north-east monsoon in October. And as the voyage took from a month to six weeks, they had little margin of time in which to make it.

This rule was carefully observed by shipping, both European and native, for many years after Caesar Frederick's day. Some sixty years later the Englishman William Methwold wrote of sailings from Masulipatam: "In September the ships for Achyne (Sumatra), Arrecan, Pegu and Tannassery (Tenasserim) set all sayle, for it is to be understood that alongst this and all other Coasts of India, the windes blow constantly trade sixe moneths one way, and sixe moneths another: which they call the Monsons alternately succeeding each other, not missing to alter in Aprill and October, only variable towards their end, so that taking the last of a Monson, they set sayles, and with a forewind arrive at their desired haven and there negotiating their affaires, they set sayle from thence in February or March following, and with the like favourable gale returns in Aprill unto their owne ports." And we know from the early eighteenth-century Fort St. George (Madras) Diaries that the rule was still in operation.

Caesar Frederick was an acute observer, and the picture he paints of the Burma he saw is so full of interest that it deserves far fuller treatment than can be given here. One would like to quote in full his vivid account of his journey up the Sittang from Martaban to Pegu, in the course of which his boat had to negotiate that river's formidable bore. The impression it made on him may be perceived from his opening sentence: "And in this voyage you shall have a Macareo, which is one of the most marvellous things in the world that nature hath wrought, and I never saw anything so hard to be beleeved as this, to wit, the great increasing and diminishing of the water there at one push or instant, and the horrible earthquake and great noyse that the said Macareo maketh where it commeth."

He went also to see an elephant hunt near Pegu and his account of it might still serve as a description of a modern hunt. He describes the king's riches with particular gusto. To the gold-hunting Europeans of his time, fired as they were by the Spanish discoveries of precious metals in America, such things had a special appeal. "This king hath divers Magasons ful of treasure, as gold and silver, and every day he encreaseth it more and more, and it is never diminished. Also he is Lord of the Mines of Rubies, Safires and Spinels. Neere unto his royal pallace there is an inestimable treasure whereof hee maketh no accompt, for it standeth in such a place that everyone may see it, and the place where this treasure is, is a great Court walled about with walls of stone, with two gates which stand open every day." He arrived there, of course, just at the time when Pegu was glutted with the loot of Ayuthia. Fitch was equally impressed with the riches he saw, but thought that far too much gold was wasted upon pagodas. "If they did not consume their gold on these vanities," he writes ruefully, "it would bee very plentiful and good cheape in Pegu."

Fitch's story of his 'wonderfull travailes' is, in spite of the defects already noted, full of interest. Not only did Hakluyt make it a feature of the second edition of his *Principall Navigations*, but Purchas also included it in his *Pilgrimes*. He left England with three companions in 1583 and returned alone in 1591, to the great surprise of his relatives, who, deeming him dead, had divided his estate according to the terms of the will, which he had executed before his departure. He parted from his companions in India and travelled farther east alone, maintaining himself by trading as opportunity offered. He sailed from Sripur in eastern Bengal at the end of November 1586 and landed at Bassein in the Delta early in 1587. He noted the houses built on 'great high postes', a custom which he decided was due to 'feare of Tygers, which be very many'. He emphasizes more than once that the country was 'very fruitfull' and the people 'very tall and well disposed'. There is nothing in his account indicating any signs of the coming collapse. He was as much impressed by Nandabayin's majesty and riches as Caesar Frederick by his predecessor's. The evidence of his reliance upon the Venetian's story is only too obvious; but from time to time he inserts passages, entirely drawn from his own reminiscences, which show that he made the most minute enquiries and was a keen observer.

His best essay at independent description is on the subject of the Buddhist monkhood. "The Tallipoies," he writes, "go very strangely apparelled with one camboline or thinne cloth next to their body of a brown colour, another of yellow doubled many times upon their shoulder: and those two be girded to them with a broad girdle: and they have a skinne of leather hanging on a string about their necks, whereupon they sit, bare-headed and barefooted: for none of them weareth shoes; with their right armes bare and a great broad sombrero or shadow in their hand to defend them in the Summer from the Sunne, and in the Winter from the raine. They keepe their feasts by the Moone: and when it is new Moone they keep their greatest feaste: and then the people send rice and other things to that kiack or church of which they be; and there all the Tallipoies doe meete which be of that Churche, and eate the vituals which are sent them. When the Tallipoies do preach, many of the people cary them gifts into the pulpit where they sit and preach. And there is one which sitteth by them to take that which the people bring. It is divided among them. They have none other ceremonies nor service that I could see, but onely preaching."

He went to see the Shwe Dagon Pagoda, which from its imposing hill site still dominates Rangoon. His description of it is too long for insertion in full, but the following extract shows how it appeared to his admiring gaze: "About two dayes journey from Pegu there is a Varelle or Pagode, which is the pilgrimage of the Pegues: it is called Dogonne, and is of a woonderfull bignesse, and all gilded from the foot to the toppe. It is the fairest place, as I suppose, that is in the world: it standeth very high, and there are foure ways to it, which all along are set with trees of fruits, in such wise that a man may go in the shade above two miles in length." Unlike Fitch, Gasparo Balbi, who, as we have seen, visited Pegu a few years earlier than the Englishman, had a conversation with King Nanda-bayin. When Balbi described his home city of Venice as a free state without a king, he records that the king was completely overcome with laughter. He thought such a notion incredible.

Until the last decade of the sixteenth century, when the Dutch and the English began to break through the ring fence of monopoly and secrecy, with which the Portuguese guarded their eastern empire, a bare handful of individual prospectors from other nations managed to penetrate as far as Burma, which in any case was far from the beaten track. How many tried and failed is not recorded. After the absorption of Portugal by Spain in 1580, the protestant nations became more and more eager to obtain a share in the rich spice trade. The earliest English voyages to the Indian Ocean, beginning with Raymond and Lancaster's in 1591, were made on the assumption that it should be possible to trade with places not under Portuguese control. Thus when the East India Company was in process of formation, it was decided to avoid all places where they were established, and for this reason Arakan, Pegu and Tenasserim were excluded from the scope of its operations. The same limitation of scope was also applied by the Company of Far Regions, formed in 1594, which financed the first Dutch voyage, that of Cornelis de Houtman to the Malay Archipelago.

The great need was for information. The capture of the carrack *Madre de Dios* in 1592 provided the English with a copy of a register of Portuguese trade and government in the East Indies. But it was a Dutchman, Jan Huyghen van Linschoten, who revolutionized the situation by publishing what almost amounted to an encylopaedia of the facts required by merchants and shippers. He arrived home in 1592 after spending six years in Goa, and devoted the rest of his life to the promotion of interest in Eastern trade. In his two works, the *Reysgeschrift* (1595) and the *Itinerario* (1596), he recorded a mass of valuable information concerning routes to the eastern seas, and the commercial products of the countries with which the Portuguese had dealings. His *Itinerario* revealed also that the Portuguese empire in the East was rotten. It was speedily translated into English, German, French and Latin, and English and Dutch merchants at once put it to practical use. It pointed particularly to Java as the best centre for the spice trade, and it was in that direction that both nations concentrated their energies during the succeeding period.

Hence, so far as the English and the Dutch were concerned, Burma and Arakan were at first completely out of the picture; and for the time being Felipe de Brito at Syriam, and the *feringhi* at Dianga, were left with a fair field for their ruffianly forays.

CHAPTER VII

ARAKAN, THE *FERINGHI* AND THE DUTCH

THAT Arakan managed to maintain itself as an independent kingdom until almost the end of the eighteenth century was mainly due to its geographical position. It was separated from Burma by a long range of mountains, the Arakan Yoma, through which there were only two practicable passes, the An connecting with Upper Burma and the Taungup connecting with Prome. The people are basically Burmese, although showing today strong traces of Indian admixture. Their language is an early form of Burmese. Writers in the past have applied to them the name Mugg (Bengali *Magh*), but the Arakanese disclaim the name and apply it only to the products of mixed marriages on the Bengal frontier. So far scholarship has failed to discover its etymology.

From very early days the older and purer form of Buddhism, the Hinayana or Lesser Vehicle, was established there. It must date from before the arrival of the Burmese in the tenth century, when Arakan was an Indian land with a population similar to that of Bengal. The Mahamuni image also, which tradition asserts to be a contemporary likeness of Gautama, is pre-Burmese though probably not earlier than the Christian era.

In the reign of Anawrahta Pagan asserted its authority over Arakan, but after 1287 this lapsed; and although before the establishment of Mrohaung by Narameikhla in 1433 there was from time to time a certain amount of Burmese and Mon interference, Arakan's contacts with Mohammedan India were probably closer than those with Burma. None of its rivers rises in Burma, and throughout its history its water communications with Bengal were much easier than its overland communications with Burma. When Bengal was strong, its rulers received the tribute of Arakan; at other times Arakan claimed tribute from parts of the Ganges delta. These fluctuations of power affected Chittagong, which was held alternatively by one side or the other. In 1459 it came into the hands of Arakan, which held it until it was finally annexed to the Mughal Empire in 1666. Mohammedanism spread to Arakan, but failed to make much impression upon its Buddhism. Mrohaung had its Sandihkan Mosque and its kings assumed Mohammedan titles, but the predominance of Buddhism was never shaken.

In the sixteenth century Arakan was a sea power of some importance; it built hundreds of galiots and developed great skill in both sea and riverine warfare. Its Chittagonian sailors lived by raiding the Ganges delta and the creeks leading up to Dacca and other towns of eastern Bengal. From about 1550 they united with the Portuguese freebooters, who settled at Dianga, the port just opposite Chittagong, and for over a century made it one of the most feared centres of piracy in the Indian seas.

The city of Mrohaung, in the Akyab district, was an eastern Venice, like modern Bangkok, a city of lagoons and canals, connected with the sea by tidal rivers. Its outer walls had a circumference of about twelve miles. Within was the palace-city, built to the same traditional pattern as Pagan and Ava and many other old capitals in Asia. The walls may still be traced today, but the palace buildings, built of teak, have long disappeared. The massive stone walls and fortifications were erected by King Minbin (1531–53) against the threat of Burmese conquest in the days of Tabinshwehti.

At the end of the century in the reign of Minyazagyi (1593–1612) the city received the vast loot brought back by its raiders from Pegu together with Nandabayin's daughter and white elephant. Pieter Willemsz van Elbing, better known in England as 'Peter Floris', was sent to Arakan in 1608 to examine the prospects of trade for the Dutch East India Company, and saw "certain portions of the treasure of Pegu, the white elephant and the king's daughter of Pegu". Apparently he advised against opening a factory at Mrohaung, because he discovered that the king really wanted naval and military assistance rather than trade.

The assistance was required against the *feringhi* of Dianga: they had become more of a liability than an asset. De Brito, who was playing his own game at Syriam, though nominally in

the service of Arakan, was suspected of planning to unite with
the Dianga pirates in conquering Arakan. To forestall this
Minyazagyi attacked the place and massacred hundreds of
feringhi. Those who escaped seized the island of Sandwip, off
the Chittagong coast, in 1609, and for some years afterwards,
under Sebastião Gonzales Tibao, carried on a most successful
policy of blackmail against Minyazagyi and his successor,
Minhkamaung (1612–22). In 1615, with forces augmented by a
fleet sent by the Viceroy of Goa, Tibao attacked Mrohaung
itself. He failed, Goa withdrew its support, and in 1617 the
Arakanese put an end to his depredations by capturing
Sandwip.

After this the *feringhi* returned to their old headquarters at
Dianga. They became once more the nominal subjects of
Arakan, and worked off their superfluous energy by annual
slave raids into Bengal. An Augustinian friar of Oporto,
Sebastião Manrique, who was appointed vicar of Dianga in
1529, has left an interesting picture of their activities in the
journal of his travels, an English translation of which was
published in 1927 by the Hakluyt Society. He says that the
feringhi brought no less than 3400 slaves annually to Dianga.
While he was there, it was rumoured that King Thirithudamma (1622–38) was planning to administer a further dose of
the medicine with which Dianga had been treated in 1607. Fra
Manrique therefore was sent to Mrohaung in 1630 to persuade
the king to call off the projected attack.

His mission was successful, and during a six-months' stay
there he got on such good terms with the king, that he obtained
permission to build a Catholic church in the suburbs of
Daingri-pet for the use of the Portuguese mercenaries serving
in the Royal Guard. He also, like Floris, saw the Pegu loot, the
white elephant and Nandabayin's daughter, then a widow and
the Grand Dowager of the Court. She herself told him, with
deep emotion, the story of her sufferings.

In 1633 Manrique was again in Mrohaung, this time as the
adviser to a Portuguese envoy sent from Goa to treat with King
Thirithudamma. His stay was a lengthy one, and in 1635 he
witnessed the long-deferred coronation of the king. In his book
he describes it in glowing colours. The book is a truly remark-

able document: it paints a vivid picture of Mrohaung in the
days of its prosperity and power.

Thirithudamma cultivated friendly relations with the Dutch
at Batavia and persuaded them to open a factory at his capital.
They were in urgent need of regular supplies of rice and slaves
for their Indonesian settlements, and could obtain large
quantities of both in Arakan. The slaves were the fruits of the
feringhi raids on Bengal. After Thirithudamma's death the
Dutch quarrelled with his successor, Narapatigyi (1638–45) and
for some years withdrew their factory. It was not reopened
until the reign of Sandathudamma (1652–84). In 1653 he signed
a commercial treaty with Batavia, which laid down the terms
upon which Dutch trade at Mrohaung was regulated for many
years. Sandathudamma is celebrated in the Arakanese chronicles as one of the noblest of their kings. During his long reign
Arakan pursued a far more enlightened policy towards European
traders than did its neighbour Burma. Unlike Burma it used
coined money. The Mughal *tanga*, the predecessor of the rupee,
was used in its ports, and from about 1660 an Arakanese
coinage, imitating that of India, was struck. For small bazaar
transactions cowrie shells were used. They were imported from
the Maldives, often by Dutch ships, which sold them in
Arakan at the rate of forty-eight viss for a rupee. The main articles
imported into the country by the Dutch were spices and
Japanese iron from Batavia, and Indian piece-goods from their
Coromandel Coast factories. The *Daghregister* of Batavia shows
that the Arakan trade was by no means an unimportant department of Dutch commerce in the Bay of Bengal.

Dutch relations with Sandathudamma were interrupted in
1665 through an incident famous in Mughal annals. Shah
Shujah, son of the Emperor Shah Jehan and Viceroy of Bengal,
was involved with his brothers in the scramble for the throne
which arose out of their father's serious illness in 1657. It was
won by Aurungzeb, who managed to secure the throne in the
following year. In 1660 Shujah, unable to hold Bengal against
his brothers' attacks, fled to Dacca and took ship for Arakan
together with his family and a great quantity of treasure. The
Dianga *feringhi* relieved him of much of the treasure before he
reached Mrohaung. His advertised plan was to make a pil-

grimage to Mecca, and Sandathudamma promised him ships
for the purpose. The Mughal government demanded his
extradition, and while the king of Arakan procrastinated,
trouble broke out. In December 1660 some of Shah Shujah's
retinue ran amok and nearly succeeded in firing the palace. The
Arakanese massacred them, and the refugee prince's own life
was only spared through the intercession of the king's mother,
who argued that it was unwise for him to teach his subjects so
dangerous a sport as that of killing princes.

Shah Shujah was then placed under restraint. In the following February there was another massacre, and he disappeared,
never to be seen again. The Dutch factors at Mrohaung were
told that he had attempted to escape from custody with the
intention of seizing the throne of Arakan, and had lost his life
in the fighting that ensued. His wives and children were taken
alive; the women were lodged in the royal harem, the princes
placed in close confinement. About two years later a desperate
attempt was made by some Mohammedans to liberate them,
and a part of the palace was set on fire. The attempt failed, the
young men were beheaded, and there was a general massacre
of Mohammedans and Bengalis in the capital. Report had it
that at the same time the Mughal princesses in the royal harem
were starved to death.

For some time before this last incident the Mughal Viceroy
of Bengal had been sending urgent messages for the surrender
of the young princes. Sandathudamma paid no attention to
them, and on the occasion of the last massacre even went so
far as to imprison a Mughal envoy. Fearing reprisals he
encouraged the *feringhi* of Dianga to redouble their efforts in
raiding Bengal. Thus in 1664 their galeasses sailed up the river
towards Dacca, broke up a Mughal flotilla of 240 vessels and
laid waste far and wide. The Mughal government therefore
decided that the pirate nest must be finally destroyed. Aurungzeb's maternal uncle, Shayista Khan, who had become Viceroy
of Bengal, prepared to make a supreme effort. Both sides needed
ships, and both plied the Dutch with insistent demands for
help. Matters came to a head in 1665. When the Dutch stub-
bornly clung to their neutrality Shayista Khan threatened to
expel them from their Bengal factories if they did not at once

evacuate Arakan. So one dark night in November of that year they loaded four ships with everything they could carry from their Mrohaung factory, and before the king of Arakan realized what was afoot, they were beyond pursuit.

Shayista Khan was already attacking the *feringhi* outposts on Sandwip Island. A few months later, in 1666, he captured and destroyed the formidable port on the mainland that for a century had wrought such devastation to the rich delta lands of the Ganges. Two thousand of the slavers were themselves sold into slavery. Others were permitted to settle as peaceful citizens at Feringhi Bazaar, twelve miles south of Dacca, where their descendants may still be found.

Arakan never recovered from this blow. The Dutch returned after a safe interval and resumed their trading; but not for long, since with the death of Sandathudamma in 1684 the country fell upon evil days. Such of Shah Shujah's followers as had escaped massacre were enrolled as Archers of the Royal Guard. They made and unmade kings at will, burnt the palace and preyed upon the land. For a brief interval under Sandawizaya (1710–31) there was some semblance of settled government. He suppressed the unruly Archers and settled them on the island of Ramree. He was strong enough to fight the Raja of Tippera and raid parts of Burma. But after his murder in 1731 anarchy once more prevailed until in 1784 Bodawpaya of Burma sent an army to seize the country, and early in the next year deposed its last king, Thamada (1782–85).

CHAPTER VIII

THE LATER TOUNGOO DYNASTY
(1600–1752)

THE dissolution of the kingdom of Tabinshwehti and Bayin-naung was only temporary. Away in the north the Nyaungyan Prince, a son of Bayinnaung, held Ava and planned to restore the monarchy of his father. In a series of preliminary cam-paigns he reduced the Shan states of Mogaung, Mohnyin, Bhamo, Mone, Yaunghwe and Hsenwi. But on the way home from Hsenwi in 1605 he died leaving his vigorous son Anaukpetlun to carry on his work. Anaukpetlun, having established his rule firmly in the north, proceeded to conquer the south. Prome fell to him in 1607, Toungoo in 1610. Then Syriam under Felipe de Brito became his chief objective.

De Brito in the meantime had been to Goa to lay his plans before the Viceroy. He received a niece of the Viceroy in marriage, the official blessing on his enterprise, and some reinforcements. During his absence the place had to withstand repeated Burmese and Arakanese attacks. At first after his return success seemed assured. In league with the Mon chief of Martaban, a vassal of Ayuthia, he began extensive military operations, made a daring and successful attack on Toungoo and challenged Anaukpetlun. But he had over-reached himself. The stranglehold which he maintained over foreign trade, by forcing it all to pass through Syriam, was strongly resented; even more so his systematic pillage of rich Buddhist shrines. With more support from Goa he still might have held out; but Goa could not afford it. In 1613 Anaukpetlun laid siege to Syriam and took it. De Brito was impaled after the Burmese fashion for criminals and died after two days of agony. His Portuguese followers were sent up country to Payeinma, and were later settled in villages between the Chindwin and Mu rivers, where for long afterwards they formed a Christian community, the *bayingyi*, with their own Catholic priests. They were enrolled in the Royal Guard as musketeers and gunners.

Some hundreds of their descendants still live in the Sagaing and Shwebo districts.

With Syriam conquered, it was possible for Anaukpetlun to turn his arms against the provinces which Ayuthia had wrested from his inheritance. He had only to appear for Martaban and the country as far south as Ye to offer its submission. But Tenasserim, defended by Siamese and Portuguese, successfully defied him, and he had to abandon the siege (1614). In the next year he turned his attention to Chiengmai, which he took. There an Englishman, Thomas Samuel, in the service of the East India Company, fell into his hands. Samuel had come East with the Company's Seventh Voyage, which had opened up trade with the Coromandel Coast and Siam. From Ayuthia he had been sent up to Chiengmai with Indian piece-goods for sale. He was well-treated by Anaukpetlun, but died soon after his arrival in Pegu. Anaukpetlun, who was anxious to establish relations with the English, sent a message by Mohammedan merchants to Masulipatam offering to restore Samuel's property to the Company, if it would open a factory in his country.

Two years later, in 1617, Henry Forrest and John Stavely were sent by William Methwold, the Company's Agent at Masulipatam, to claim the dead man's estate. They were well received by the king; but when he realized that they had not come to establish regular trading relations, he held them as hostages, hoping thereby to force the Company's hand. After three years, however, he packed them off back to Masulipatam with a present for the Agent, the remainder of Samuel's goods and a letter written on palm leaf offering 'free trade' to English merchants. Their behaviour in Pegu had been so discreditable that Methwold sent them under arrest to the Company's head factory at Jaccatra in Java, whence they were shipped home to be summarily dismissed by their employers. Apparently they had gambled away the proceeds of a consignment of goods, with which they had been provided for sale in Pegu, and had brought back a false set of accounts. Their adverse report on trading prospects in Burma led the Masulipatam factory to fight shy of opening up trade there for many years.

The assistance given by the Portuguese to Siam in the

defence of Tenasserim caused Anaukpetlun some apprehension lest his enemies, Ayuthia and Arakan, might prevail on
them to seek to avenge the death of de Brito. Accordingly he
sent a mission to Goa to excuse his act and offer the restoration
of his Portuguese prisoners. But when a Goanese envoy,
Martin de Costa Falcam, promptly appeared at his court to
talk business, he refused to receive him. The only explanation
of this surprising *volte face* seems to be that after sending his
mission he must have heard, presumably from Muslim merchants, of the rich harvest of Portuguese prizes that the Dutch
were beginning to reap on their onslaught on the spice islands,
and to have decided that there was nothing to fear from them.

Although Ava had been the base from which Anaukpetlun
had started out to regain the kingdom of his fathers, Pegu
became his headquarters in his later years. He planned to renew
the struggle with Ayuthia. In 1628 he transferred the remainder of his household from Ava to Pegu. But a palace intrigue cut short his plans and he was murdered. After a brief
interval of civil war, one of his brothers, Thalun, seized the
throne and was crowned at Pegu. His reign of nineteen years
(1629-48) contains one event of supreme importance in
Burmese history. In 1635 he abandoned Pegu and transferred
his capital to Ava. Henceforward Ava, or some other site close
by, was to be the capital until the final collapse of the kingdom in
1885.

The motives inspiring the move are not difficult to detect. A
fairly considerable Mon revolt occurred immediately after
Thalun's coronation. When it was repressed, another Mon
exodus to Siam resulted, and Ayuthia resisted the Burmese
demand for their surrender. Unlike his predecessors, Thalun
decided against a war with Siam: peace and stabilization were
his policy. In Burmese eyes Pegu possessed few advantages as a
capital save as a base for attacking Siam. By 1600 Pegu had
become useless as a port through silting. Syriam had taken its
place, and in many ways would have proved a better capital
than Ava. But the Mons were disaffected, and the Delta was
depopulated and exposed to attack. Moreover no Burmese king
of this period had any real appreciation of the value of overseas
intercourse.

E

There was another factor not without its influence: the move was made at a time when all the countries round the Bay of Bengal were in the grip of one of the worst famines on record. The Dutch, who came to Burma late in the year 1634 to negotiate trading terms, reported that the whole country was famine-stricken, people were dying of starvation and trade was at a standstill. This alone would suffice to explain the decision to abandon an expansionist policy and seek safety in retrenchment.

So the idea of a national kingship by union with the Mons was forsaken, a fresh coronation on strictly Burmese lines was held in the new capital, and in Harvey's words, "the court relapsed into its tribal homeland, Upper Burma". It was a retrograde step, a surrender to traditionalism. Four hundred miles was a long way from the sea in those days. The journey up-stream from Syriam to Ava often took as much as two months. Thus, cut off from contact with the outside world, Burmese rulers came truly to believe that their palace was the centre of the universe, that building pagodas, collecting daughters from vassals, and raiding their neighbours for white elephants and slaves was the essence of kingcraft. It is not without significance that Siam, which, when forced in the next century to evacuate its capital, built one at a seaport rather than further inland, managed to survive as an independent state, while Burma succumbed to foreign conquest. The chief ingredient in the failure of the Burmese kingdom was supplied not by 'Western Imperialism', but by the intransigence and xenophobia which radiated from the Court of Ava.

Apart from the Mon revolt at its commencement, Thalun's reign was peaceful. He aimed at restoring order and social organization. His minister, Kaingsa, compiled the first law book in Burmese, the *Manusarashwemin* or *Maharaja dhamma-that*. It owed much to earlier Mon collections, but substituted Burmese ideas on inheritance for the Hindu ideas on which Mon law was based. Thalun also reconstructed the administration of the Kyauksè irrigation area. Regiments of the army were settled there as tenants. With the Court once more established at Ava this area naturally resumed its earlier importance.

Thalun's greatest work, however, was to overhaul the revenue administration of the whole kingdom. Under his direction the Revenue Inquest of 1638 was carried out, and what must have been a sort of Domesday Book compiled. Unfortunately none of it has survived, and all that is known of it comes from references to it in the later compilations undertaken in Bodawpaya's reign. Thalun was the last king of his line with real ability. But his unenlightened conservatism promoted a sterile stability which was the enemy of progress.

It was in Thalun's reign that both the Dutch and the English East India Companies planted their first factories in Burma. In September 1635 he received the Dutch factors, Dirck Steur and Wiert Jansen Popta, at his new capital, and treated them to 'sundry spectacles of dancing, leaping and fighting'. They reported that his palace was very elegant, and that at their official reception he sat for nearly two hours on his throne without uttering a word. The *Daghregister* of Batavia contains the translation of a letter written by him in reply to one from the Governor of Pulicat complaining of trading losses.

In his letter he tells the Dutch that their troubles are due to the competition of Indian traders and to their failure to understand Burmese business methods. He in his turn complains that their hostility to the Portuguese is preventing the latter from carrying on their accustomed trade with his kingdom. His letter incidentally contains a list of the articles he is willing to export, namely rubies, gold, lac, tin, long pepper, wax, deer pelts and buffaloes' horns.

The Dutch were so deeply disappointed in the trade that they thought of closing their factories at Syriam and Ava. In 1645 they threatened to do so, but did not carry out their threat because they feared that the English would step into their shoes. Two years later the English did indeed plant a factory in Burma, their first. Fort St. George, Madras, was its parent, Masulipatam having refused to have any share in the venture. It lasted less than ten years. Dutch competition was one of the chief causes of its failure.

After Thalun the remaining kings of his dynasty were nonentities; each was weaker than his predecessor. Pindale (1648-1661) was helpless before the ravages of Chinese freebooter armies, the backwash of the civil war in China which

accompanied the fall of the Ming dynasty. Yung-li, the last of
the Mings, driven out in 1644 by the Manchus, fled to Yunnan,
where for some years he held out gallantly. His excessive
demands on some of the neighbouring Shan states for men and
supplies caused them to appeal to Burma for help. When Pindale sent a force, the Chinese began to raid Burmese territory.
Their raids were mentioned in reports sent to Madras by the
English factors at Ava. In 1658 Yung-li was finally defeated in
Yunnan and fled by the old Burma Road to Bhamo. He and his
followers were disarmed and permitted to reside at Sagaing,
near the capital, where they were kept under the closest restraint.
The result was more raids, this time by bands of Ming sup-
porters endeavouring to rescue their leader. They defeated a
Burmese army at Wetwin, and for three years ravaged Upper
Burma right up to the walls of Ava. In 1661 the Dutch reported
that their raids were causing so much confusion that all trade
had stopped. For a time they controlled the Kyauksè area and
caused starvation in Ava.

At the same time Pindale became involved in serious
trouble in the south. Mon levies, called to the help of the capital,
deserted, and Martaban rose in revolt. Then, fearing reprisals,
some thousands of Mons fled over the border into Siam. A
Burmese force, sent after them, met with disaster at the hands
of the Siamese at Kanburi beyond the Three Pagodas Pass; and
the Siamese, taking advantage of the weakness of Ava, proceeded
to raid Pegu and other places in Lower Burma. So serious was
the situation that the Dutch had to take special measures for
the protection of their factory at Syriam. In the midst of the
confusion a court intrigue dethroned the weak Pindale and
placed his brother Pye (1661–72) on the throne.

The Chinese raids continued for some months after Pye's
accession. But they soon died down, largely because Yunnan,
their base, was denied them by the energetic mopping-up
measures of the Manchus. In 1662 Sankuei, the Viceroy of
Yunnan, marched into Burma and delivered an ultimatum
demanding the surrender of Yung-li. Pye, powerless to resist,
handed over the refugee, who was carried off to Yunnan Fu and
publicly strangled with a bow-string in the market-place. This
crowning humiliation caused a rumour to circulate that Ava

was doomed. According to the Dutch the king was urged to transfer his capital to another site. In 1663 he held a grand council to discuss the matter, but against the opinion of the majority rejected the proposal on the grounds that his people were too impoverished by raids and warfare for him to impose such a heavy additional burden on them.

With the surrender of Yung-li quiet settled once more upon the country and trade began to revive. The reports of the Dutch became more optimistic, and when they learnt that the capital was not to be moved they decided to spend money on renovating their factory there. The Siamese raids also ceased. While Burma lay helpless before the Chinese threat, they had recovered Chiengmai, which Anaukpetlun had taken in 1615. Pye was too weak to attempt its recovery and the old feud between the two states died down for the time being. There were, of course, occasional forays, but nothing of importance.

From this time onwards until the great Mon revolt of 1740 the history of Burma is a record of stagnation. Minrekyawdin (1673–98) was a puppet, entirely in the hands of his ministers. The Dutch quarrelled with him over the restrictions placed on their trade and in 1679 withdrew their factories, having finally decided that trade with his country was not a paying proposition. Thereupon the English Company, urged on by James, Duke of York, began once more to show some interest in Burma, and commenced negotiations for the reopening of the factories it had abandoned in the days of Cromwell. It was arming its Indian settlements and required saltpetre for the manufacture of gunpowder. Moreover, Europeans in the East were becoming aware of the fact that Burma possessed rich teak forests. Their trading stations on the Coromandel Coast were importing large consignments of teak timber through private merchants, who shipped it at Syriam.

After desultory negotiations over some years, however, the East India Company decided not to reopen its factories. The king returned evasive answers to its proposals for a trade agreement, and was decidedly averse to any trade in saltpetre. He had already resisted strong pressure on the part of the Dutch to be permitted to manufacture gunpowder in Burma. Hence the English came to the conclusion that they could obtain all the

Burma products they needed through the operations of private
merchants, and Madras adopted the practice of issuing special
licences to European residents to engage in trading voyages to
Syriam. In this way a brisk trade developed between the two
ports.

The revival of English interest in Burma began in 1680, the
year after the Dutch withdrawal. But the removal of Dutch
competition was not its chief cause, notwithstanding the fact
that a Dutchman, named Spar, who claimed to have been the
chief of the Dutch factory at Ava, journeyed to London, while
Madras was considering the question, and persuaded James,
Duke of York, that Burma offered an excellent base for opening
up trade with China overland. The real cause was the spectacular attempt of Louis XIV of France to gain control over Siam.

After its first failure in Burma the East India Company had
transferred its interest to Siam, where it had opened a factory
in 1661. Siam offered far better trading terms than Burma.
By 1680, however, owing to French influence and the hostility
of the ambitious minister, Constant Phaulkon, the English
factory at Ayuthia had fallen upon evil days. The withdrawal of
the Dutch from Burma thus offered the English an opportunity
to renew relations with Ava as a counterpoise for failure in Siam.

By 1686, when it was obvious that nothing could be gained
by reopening the old factory at Syriam, a new plan of quite a
different nature presented itself to the Madras Council. This
was nothing less than the seizure of the island of Negrais, inside
the mouth of the Bassein river on the extreme south-west of
the Irrawaddy delta. Strictly speaking, the project had no
connection with the Burma negotiations; it formed part of a
policy of reprisals against Siam, into which the Company had
been goaded by the piratical acts of a number of renegade
Englishmen, who used the port of Mergui as their base. The
Company wanted a safe harbour on the east side of the Bay of
Bengal, from which it could threaten Mergui and other piratical
bases in the Tenasserim area. The strategical value of such a
place might become even higher, should France, as then seemed
only too likely, achieve political domination over Siam. Incidentally, the Madras Council, when the matter was discussed,
thought that the island belonged to Arakan, not to Burma.

The project was never carried through. The expedition could not be equipped in time to sail before the change of monsoon made voyages to the Burma coast impracticable, and it was called off. News of it came, however, to the ears of Samuel White, Maurice Collis's 'Siamese White', at Mergui, and he was so alarmed that he sent a small Siamese force to occupy the island; but Constant Phaulkon himself at once countermanded this rash act, and early in 1687 the troops were withdrawn.

Meanwhile the Directors of the Company in London had persuaded James II to write a personal letter to the English at Megui, proposing that they should surrender the port to an English frigate as a counter-stroke to the Grand Monarque's despatch of troops and artificers to Siam under the Maréchal Des Farges. This plan also miscarried. Before the letter arrived, the Siamese at Mergui had risen and slaughtered every English-man they could lay hands on. One of the survivors, a certain Captain Anthony Weltden of the ship *Curtana*, sailed away to the island of Negrais, where he destroyed some inscriptions, which White's force had set up, claiming the place for Siam, and before leaving erected others claiming it for England.

There the matter ended. No claim was ever made to the island on the score of Weltden's visit. The Company had be-come involved in a quarrel with Aurungzeb, the Great Mughal, and could spare no further attention to the plan for developing a naval station across the Bay. And it soon became evident that French policy in Siam had badly overreached itself, so that there was no longer any need for such a station.

The decision of the Company not to reopen its Syriam factory disappointed the Court of Afva. In the hope of forcing the Company's hand the Burmese seized an Armenian merchant of Madras and his ship, forced through stress of weather to enter the port of Martaban. As luck would have it, part of the cargo belonged to Nathaniel Higginson, the Governor of Madras, who was therefore impelled to send over an envoy to request the liberation of the captive merchant and his property. Dalrymple in his *Oriental Repertory* prints the diary of Edward Fleetwood, the agent entrusted with this task.

Now Higginson was well aware that only if he could promise that official trading relations would be established,

would his request be granted. He therefore did his best to pass
off the mission as an official one, sent with that object by the
East India Company. It was nothing of the kind. Fleetwood
himself was a private merchant, not a Company's servant, and
his expenses were paid by Higginson out of his own pocket.

The Court of Ava was distinctly suspicious that there was a
catch somewhere; it 'insisted mightily' that the Syriam factory
must be officially reopened. Eventually it was arranged that the
Company should have a dock for shipbuilding there under
the charge of a duly-appointed Chief. The difficulty was,
however, that the Company would not allow itself to be officially committed to the venture. Higginson tried to form a small
private syndicate to take over the business, but could get no
support. Ultimately he solved the problem by appointing a
Chief from among the Madras merchants trading to Syriam,
and giving him authority over the rest. The 'Chief of the
Affairs of the English Nation' was empowered to take over the
Company's old factory site as his headquarters and hoist the
English flag. Actually he was a private shipwright resident in
Madras, who went out with the Madras shippers in September
each year and returned with them in the following March.

This arrangement lasted until 1720, when as the result of
the Chief, George Heron, becoming implicated in a very un-
savoury murder case, he was superseded by a regular Resident.
The new official was a private contractor, who had to pay down
a large sum as security money to the Madras Council, reside
permanently at Syriam and undertake the construction and
repair of ships for the Company. The French employed a
similar method there at the same time. Both companies were
becoming increasingly interested in the Burma teak trade, and
with the development of their naval rivalry, Syriam began to
enter into their strategic calculations. The experiment, however, was a failure; the work was badly executed and expensive,
and by the time the great Mon revolt began in 1740, the
Madras Council had decided to transfer its shipbuilding
orders to the more efficient Parsi yards at Bombay. In 1743
the Mons burnt the English factory to the ground, and the last
Resident, Jonathan Smart, was withdrawn.

During these years the Toungoo dynasty was represented

by three weak kings, Sane (1698–1714), Taninganwe (1714–33) and Mahadammayaza Dipati (1733–1752). Ever since the move to Ava in 1635 the atmosphere of the Court had become closer and its outlook more restricted. Kings rarely left the capital; they became practically palace prisoners, surrounded by all the jealousies and intrigues of harem life. Tradition prescribed that the chief queen must be the king's half-sister. Their children, together with those of lesser queens, were numbered in scores, and all lived in frightful apprehension of the fact that when their father died, a mad scramble for the throne was likely to break out, resulting in a blood bath of all considered dangerous to the successful candidate.

How much actual control Ava exercised over its dominions at this time it is difficult to say. The country was divided into appanages, many of which were held by members of the royal family. From among them at any moment a *minlaung*, or pretender to the throne, might arise, who would rally the disorderly elements of his district around him in an attempt to seize power. Even when unsuccessful, as most were, they terrorized the countryside with dacoity. It is doubtful if these later kings of the Toungoo dynasty had any control over Lower Burma beyond the Irrawaddy highway, the city of Pegu and the port of Syriam. In any case the devastation of the Delta region in Bayinnaung's reign and the exodus of thousands of Mons, had created a wilderness from which little was to be feared for many years afterwards. But in the eighteenth century the weakness of the Ava kingship was so obvious that there was bound to come a time when the Mons would dream of restoring the old kingdom of Pegu.

It was the little trans-Chindwin mountain state of Manipur which laid bare the full weakness of Ava. This kingdom of expert horsemen, whose national sport was forty-a-side polo, had been made tributary by Bayinnaung in the sixteenth century. Subsequently it had reverted to independence, and had occasionally raided Burmese territory. Under Gharib Newaz (1714–54) its raids became chronic and far-reaching. The Manipuris had become converted to Hinduism, and were incited by their Brahmins to seek blessedness by bathing in the Irrawaddy at Sagaing. In time their raids came right up to the

walls of Ava, and Burmese garrisons, planted on the Upper
Chindwin, were unable to stop them. In 1749 Gharib Newaz
only just failed to take Ava.

The monarchy was doomed. Already, in 1740, the Mons
had proclaimed their independence and installed their own
king at Pegu. Elsewhere *minlaungs* were springing up and
dacoity was rife. By 1750 the situation had become so critical
that Mahadammayaza Dipati in despair sent envoys to Yunnan
begging for help. In April 1752 a Mon column forced its way
into Ava, burnt the city to the ground and deported the king and
the royal family as prisoners to Pegu.

CHAPTER IX

THE MON REVOLT

THE Mon revolt, which brought about the downfall of the Toungoo dynasty, was an act of desperation. It was not a carefully planned national rising, but arose out of the chaos produced by the Court of Ava's failure to cope with the Manipuri raids. It was in 1738 that they first galloped past the Upper Chindwin stockades to carry fire and sword up to the very walls of Ava. The old door of the eastern entrance to the Kaunghmudaw Pagoda still bears marks said to have been made by the sword of Gharib Newaz as he forced his way in to slaughter its garrison. In such a situation revolt was bound to ensue. It began in 1740 with a colony of Gwe Shans at Okpo near Madaya, not many miles away from the capital. They were discontented because of the exorbitant taxes demanded on their areca palms. So, under the leadership of a *minlaung* Gonna-ein, they united with a band of Mon deportees settled at Madaya and drove the Burmese out of their district.

Almost at the same time the Burmese governor of Pegu also turned *minlaung*, demanded the allegiance of Lower Burma, and marched on Syriam. But his troops mutinied and killed him, and when the king sent his uncle down to restore order, the Mons rose *en masse*, murdered him and massacred the Burmese in Syriam and Martaban. They proceeded to invest as their king the son of a rebel governor of Pagan, who claimed royal descent. The father had failed in an attempt on the throne in 1714 and had taken refuge in the inhospitable hill country to the east of Pegu. His son was a monk when he was proclaimed king of Pegu with the title of Smim Htaw Buddhaketi. He was, however, only a puppet in the hands of a Mon leader, Binnya Dala.

Profiting by the weakness of Ava, the Mons quickly made themselves masters of Prome and Toungoo, and were soon raiding up the Irrawaddy as far as the capital itself. Smim Htaw Buddhaketi was anxious to establish good relations with

the European traders in Syriam and offered Jonathan Smart,
the English Resident, the post of Shabunder, or Controller of
the Port. But the Madras Council sternly commanded him to
maintain strict neutrality, and sent him a small guard of sepoys
for the better security of the factory.

In 1743 the situation suddenly changed. The Burmese
raided into the heart of the Mon country and seized Syriam.
In the course of a three-days' sack they burnt the Portuguese,
Armenian and French churches there, and destroyed all the
warehouses of foreign merchants except the English factory,
which was apparently saved by its handful of sepoys. The Mons,
however, counter-attacked just when the Burmese, demoralized
by plunder, were too drunk to resist, and recovered the town.
Smart's attempt at neutrality was interpreted as a sign of
sympathy with the Burmese. He was compelled to surrender,
and the factory was burnt to the ground. He and his company,
however, were allowed to leave for Madras without further
molestation.

In the same year an Italian Barnabite priest, Father Gallizia,
who had received papal consecration as first Bishop of Burma,
arrived at Syriam en route for Ava with a small band of assistant
clergy. Finding it impossible to travel up to the capital, he made
his way to Pegu, where he was well received. Some time later
six ships belonging to the Ostend Company arrived in Syriam
harbour. The Company's factors had been expelled from
Bankibazar in Bengal and had come in the expectation of
obtaining permission to establish trade with Burma. Gallizia
was requested by the Governor of Syriam to ascertain their
intentions. He prevailed upon their leader, de Schonamille, to
go with him to lay his case before the Mon king at Pegu. De
Schonamille took with him a considerable escort, thereby
rousing Mon suspicions to such a pitch that a plot was formed
to massacre the whole party. Becoming aware of what was
afoot, Gallizia warned de Schonamille, who made a desperate
effort to escape. But he and all his suite, together with the
bishop and two priests, were surrounded and butchered almost
to a man. The ships with four survivors of the massacre managed to make good their escape from Syriam.

Smim Htaw Buddhaketi proved an ineffectual king: he

spent most of his time searching the jungles for a white elephant. In 1747 his ministers decided that their cause demanded a real leader and in his stead raised Binnya Dala to the throne. Under him the Mon raids into the distracted Kingdom of Ava became more and more insistent until at last, having seized the vital Kyauksè area, they besieged Ava, and in April 1752 the city fell.

It looked as if the Mons had at last turned the tables on the Burmese. Detachments were sent out in all directions to administer the water of allegiance. The Einshemin or Heir Apparent, Binnya Dala's younger brother, evidently thought that all resistance was at an end. He prepared to ship the main body of his troops downstream, leaving a garrison behind under his next-in-command, Talaban. Before leaving he received the unpleasant news that one of his detachments, sent to demand the allegiance of the town of Moksobomyo ('the town of the hunter chief'), about forty miles north of Ava, had been cut to pieces by the inhabitants. He ought to have enquired more carefully into the nature of the incident, but made the fatal mistake of treating it as trivial. With the parting injunction to Talaban to make an example of the place, he set off home with his troops.

The quarter from which he feared trouble was not Upper Burma but Siam, which had given hospitality to the Burmese governors of Martaban and Tavoy, when they fled from their rebellious subjects, and had exchanged missions and presents with Ava before its fall. Unfortunately for the Mons the resistance of Moksobomyo was the beginning of a Burmese national movement, which was to destroy the kingdom of Pegu utterly, and the thugyi of the place, who organized the resistance, was to become one of the greatest heroes in his country's history.

CHAPTER X

ALAUNGPAYA

AUNGZEYA, 'the Victorious', myothugyi of Shwebo, to give his home town its more modern name, was thirty-eight years of age, when he suddenly sprang into prominence as the Burmese national leader against the Mons. He had begun to organize his district for resistance before the fall of Ava. When he destroyed the Mon detachment, he was at the head of the combined forces of no less than forty-six villages. The Mon force sent to avenge this affront he ambushed and routed. Talaban then realized that he was up against a serious revolt. He therefore despatched as strong a force as he could spare to wipe out the centre of resistance. But the Burmese leader completely defeated it and captured all its equipment. This victory made him a *minlaung*; he claimed royal descent. He was no longer a mere resistance leader, but an aspirant to royal power. From far and wide other leaders, who had formed centres of resistance, flocked to his standard. Everywhere he went, he exacted the oath of allegiance. At Shwebo he built a palace in the traditional style, thus adding another to the list of capital cities in Upper Burma. He was now King Alaungpaya.

After his initial successes, however, he had no easy task in clearing the Mons from Upper Burma; and but for the unaccountable ineptitude of their rulers in Pegu his difficulties might indeed have been formidable. Not until the end of 1753 was he in a position to attack Ava. Then success again came with startling suddenness. Having failed in a number of sorties, the Mons lost heart, evacuated Ava by night, and fled down the Irrawaddy (January 1754).

Even then Alaungpaya was not out of the wood. While he was celebrating his victory by a round of festivities at famous pagodas, a Mon army, strong enough to have turned the scale earlier, appeared before Ava, and, though unable to storm it, wrought havoc throughout the countryside for many miles. When at last it was driven off, events occurred in the south which showed that all was not well with the Mon kingdom. A plot to liberate the captive Mahadammayaza Dipati was discovered at Pegu. Among the victims of the wholesale executions which followed were the unhappy ex-king and three of his sons, all of whom were ceremonially drowned. It was forbidden to shed royal blood.

Then at Prome the Burmese rose and drove out the Mon garrison, only to be besieged by the retreating Mon army coming downstream from Ava. But Alaungpaya was hot on the track of the Mons, and after heavy fighting drove them off from the city (February 1755). This victory secured him the allegiance of all central Burma. But he allowed the Mons no respite; he pressed on southwards and at Lunshe in Henzada district inflicted on them a decisive defeat. To celebrate it he changed the name of the place to Myanaung, 'Speedy Victory'. His advance now became a triumph. Toungoo, Henzada, Myaung-mya, Bassein and even the Arakanese district of Sandoway sent tokens of submission and allegiance. The lightning campaign ended just before the beginning of the rainy season at Dagon, which he cleared of Mons and renamed Rangoon, 'the End of Strife'.

Complete success, however, was by no means assured. As with the Mon conquest of Ava, there was no guarantee that the Burmese could hold permanently the vast territories which had fallen to them so rapidly. Pegu, the Mon capital, and Syriam, just across the river from Rangoon, still held out firmly. And at Syriam the Mons were aided by a brilliant Frenchman, the Sieur de Bruno, who had come to Burma from Pondicherry some years before as Dupleix's agent with ambitious plans for the extension of French influence.

As far back as 1727 Dupleix had written a 'Mémoire' on the subject of the French position in the Indian Ocean. In it he had drawn attention to Burma's supplies of teak and crude oil, and had recommended the use of Burmese ports for shipbuilding. Two years later, as a result of his efforts, a French shipyard was founded at Syriam, which proceeded to build some useful ships for Pondicherry. The Mon revolt, however, caused its abandonment in 1742. Not until six years later, when the War of the Austrian Succession ended, was Dupleix free to direct his

attention again to Burma. Then, when he was casting round for
fresh vantage points, from which to attack his English rivals, a
Mon envoy appeared at Pondicherry to solicit his aid against the
Burmese. He promised men and munitions; and, as a preliminary step, sent the Sieur de Bruno to examine the situation. Bruno
arrived at Pegu in July 1751. Soon afterwards he wrote to his
chief that with a few hundred well-disciplined French troops it
would be an easy matter to gain control over the Irrawaddy
delta; and Dupleix wrote home pressing for the necessary
military support to undertake the project.

Governor Saunders of Madras, ever on the watch to circum-
vent Dupleix's designs, heard rumours of a French plan to
intervene in Burma. His information pointed to a possible
occupation of the island of Negrais, and he wrote at once to
the Directors urging that the East India Company should forestall the French by seizing the place. As soon as he learnt of
Bruno's mission to Pegu, without waiting for a reply from
London, he despatched a small expedition under Captain
Thomas Taylor to survey the island. He also invested Robert
Westgarth, a private trader at Syriam, with the title of Resident,
and commissioned him to negotiate with the Mons for its cession.

Taylor found the local officials so hostile that, after a brief
and cursory survey, he went on to Pegu to add his weight to
Westgarth's solicitations. The Mon government doggedly
opposed any form of settlement at Negrais. Bruno's influence
was supreme, and he had a firm ally in the Heir Apparent, who
was reported to be the dominant personality in the government.
The Englishmen were up against a brick wall.

News of this reached Thomas Saunders in March 1753.
Meanwhile Taylor had reported adversely on Negrais: it was
useless as a trading station and decidedly unhealthy. On
receiving this report he was somewhat embarrassed to hear
from the Directors that they enthusiastically supported the plan
to occupy the island. But as soon as he heard that Bruno was so
high in favour at Pegu, he threw off all hesitation and sent a
strong expedition, which on 26 April, 1753, took possession of
the island.

It was a mistaken move. Dupleix had never been in a position
to plant a settlement there. At almost the same time as Saunders

had sent his expedition across the Bay, Dupleix had received a
letter from his director totally rejecting his ambitious scheme
to gain control over the Irrawaddy delta. Such a prohibition
would have meant little to him, had he been able to dis-
pose of adequate forces for such a purpose. But he was too
deeply involved in the Carnatic and elsewhere to disregard
his injunctions.

Right from the start the new settlement was a serious
liability. Disease took a terrible toll, and the Mons boycotted it
so successfully that all its supplies of food and labour had to be
brought across from Madras. But there could be no thought of
evacuation while Bruno remained at the Court of Pegu. At the
end of the year 1753, however, the outlook for the English
began to be a little more hopeful. The rise of Alaungpaya and
the Mon abandonment of Ava offered a better opportunity for
bargaining. Even Dupleix became undecided as to whether he
were backing the right horse, and went so far as to despatch some
boatloads of much-needed arms and ammunition to Alaungpaya.
And the Mons, growing suspicious of their French ally, sent
envoys to Madras promising the cession of Negrais in return for
military support.

Nothing came of these manœuvres. When Thomas Saunders presented the Mons with a treaty for signature, the old
objections were again raised, and it soon became evident that
Dupleix's stock had risen even higher with the Mons because of
his gesture towards Alaungpaya. Late in 1754 Thomas Taylor
returned to Madras with the advice that English policy should
be directed towards cultivating friendly relations with Alaungpaya. When, therefore, the Burmese champion, in the course
of his campaign down the Irrawaddy, sent envoys to Negrais
(March 1755), they were cordially received, and the Company's
Agent, Henry Brooke, wrote to Madras urging military intervention on the side of the Burmese.

George Pigot had by now succeeded Thomas Saunders as
Governor of Madras. Seeing a new struggle with the French
looming upon the Indian horizon he wisely decided to spare no
troops for a further wild-goose chase in Burma. The Negrais
post had become a serious financial liability and the prospects of
profitable trade with Burma seemed extremely remote.

F

Meanwhile Alaungpaya had reached Dagon and was sending
urgent messages to Negrais asking for guns and ammunition.
Equally urgent requests for help were reaching Pondicherry
from Bruno and the Mon Heir Apparent, who were organizing
the defence of Syriam. Alaungpaya was in a fix. His equipment
was inadequate for an attack on the Mon port. Moreover, there
were difficulties in the north, which necessitated his return to
his capital. The Manipuris were raiding, the Shans were
restless, and a member of the old Toungoo royal family was
threatening to invade from Siamese territory.

Before starting on his journey upstream Alaungpaya sent
a second embassy to Negrais, and Henry Brooke decided that
the only safe course lay in a treaty giving formal recognition to
the British possession of the island in return for a promise of
military stores. So Captain George Baker was sent to follow the
king up to Shwebo with a draft treaty, identical with the one
rejected by the Mons, and a handsome present of cannon.

Baker found the king in a very angry mood. He had heard
that some English trading vessels, including a Company's ship,
the *Arcot*, had joined with the French and Mons of Syriam in
attacking the Burmese garrison at Rangoon. Baker completely
failed to shake his conviction that Henry Brooke had double-
crossed him. But the present of cannon mollified him, and,
although refusing to set his seal to such a thing as a treaty, he
signified his willingness to consider the grant of trading privi-
leges at Negrais and Bassein. It was left that the negotiations
were to be resumed after Alaungpaya's return to Rangoon.

During a brief stay at Shwebo the king with the greatest
energy tackled the problems which had caused him to suspend
operations in the south. A punitive expedition against Manipur
wrought such havoc that it is referred to in Manipuri records
as the 'first devastation'. It was to be followed by many others.
A strong detachment went to the Shan states and received
tokens of submission from most of them. Alaungpaya was also
accorded official recognition by the Viceroy of Yunnan. Then
having mustered a large additional force of Shan and Chin
levies, he returned to Rangoon to direct operations against
Syriam.

There he was met early in 1756 by Ensign John Dyer and

Dr. William Anderson, who came from Negrais to continue the negotiations begun by Captain George Baker. There were two difficulties. In the first place anything of the nature of a treaty was repugnant to Burmese conceptions of sovereignty; no king could bind his successors, or himself, for that matter. In the second place, kings only dealt with kings: it was impossible to conclude an agreement with a mere trading company. Alaungpaya was willing to give formal recognition to the Company's settlement in his country, but only by a royal order directed to the king of England. Accordingly the English envoys were entrusted with a letter on gold-leaf ornamented with rubies and told to deliver it to their king.

This interesting document arrived in England early in 1758 and was duly presented to George II. A translation of it is preserved in the East India Company's records in London. Unfortunately, when it arrived, the Directors had already sent out orders to Madras for the abandonment of the Negrais settlement. And as—still more unfortunately—no suitable reply was ever made on behalf of the king of England, Alaungpaya came to the conclusion that he had been either craftily tricked or wantonly insulted.

Meanwhile Syriam had fallen. It was taken by a surprise attack in July 1756 and utterly destroyed. Upon Bruno and the French who fell into his hands Alaungpaya wreaked a fearful revenge. Bruno was slowly roasted to death. Two French ships which arrived in the Rangoon river just too late with reinforcements and supplies from Pondicherry, were decoyed and captured through a letter, which the king forced the wretched Bruno to write to their captains before his execution. Their officers were all butchered and their companies impressed into the Burmese army.

Then, reinforced by European guns and gunners, Alaungpaya proceeded to invest the Mon capital Pegu. He sent request after request for munitions to Negrais, threatening that if the response were inadequate he would treat the settlement in the same way as Syriam. The English were now placed in a very difficult position. The Seven Years' War had broken out, and their hands were full with operations against the French. On the other hand, with the elimination of French influence in Burma, the Negrais settlement no longer had the slightest use. George Pigot had already advised London to sanction its abandonment. His report went before the Directors in March 1757, and they at once issued orders for complete withdrawal from Burma. Before these arrived, however, Alaungpaya had made a holocaust of Pegu (May 1757), and had sent peremptory orders to Negrais for its Chief to attend on him at Prome, while on his way back to the capital.

The Chief, Captain Thomas Newton, deemed it unwise to go in person, and deputed Ensign Thomas Lester to go, taking with him the best present the settlement could afford. Lester was conducted to the Burmese flotilla, as it triumphantly made its way upstream with the captive Court of Pegu and vast booty. He was accorded two interviews by Alaungpaya on the royal barge, and in his journal, which Dalrymple prints in full in his *Oriental Repertory*, has left an entertaining account of his experiences.

He had to enter the royal presence minus sword and shoes, and to hold himself throughout in a kneeling posture. The king, however, was in a good humour, and when the uncomfortable envoy sought to ease his cramped limbs by surreptitiously drawing a low stool towards him, his discomfort evoked roars of laughter, and he was graciously told to sit down in the English fashion. In accordance with his instructions Lester asked for a treaty. To this the king rejoined that the order inscribed on a gold plate, which he had sent to the king of England was sufficient guarantee. After some further argument he said in an offhand manner that if Lester insisted on a treaty, he might have one.

Throughout the discussion he plied the perplexed, and somewhat amused, Englishman with all manner of irrelevant questions. He asked why the English did not tattoo their bodies like the Burmese, and proudly exposed his own tattooed thighs. He also enquired if the English were afraid of the French; and when Lester proudly proclaimed that no Englishman had ever been born who was afraid of a Frenchman, he capped the remark by asserting that he was afraid of no one in the whole world: even if all the powers of the world were to invade his country, he could drive them out.

So they parted and went on their respective ways, the king
back to Shwebo and Lester back to Negrais with a 'treaty' in
his pocket. By it the king of Burma ceded the island of Negrais,
and granted a piece of land for a factory at Bassein, while the
Company undertook to present him annually with a twelve-
pounder cannon and 200 viss of gunpowder, and to aid him
against all his enemies by land and sea. Dalrymple prints it
verbatim in his *Oriental Repertory*. Aitchison pointedly omits
it from his monumental collection of East India Company's
treaties.

When the royal seal was affixed to the document, an order
from the Directors was on its way to Madras for the abandonment of the Burma enterprise. Soon after its arrival, the French
under Lally began to threaten Madras so seriously that Fort St.
George had to hand over relations with Burma to Fort
William in Bengal. It was Calcutta, therefore, that arranged the
evacuation of Captain Thomas Newton and the main garrison of
Negrais in April 1759. A good deal of timber and stores could
not be carried away at the time, and was left there under a small
guard.

During the cold season, just before this move, Alaungpaya
led another great raid into Manipur. His absence was the
signal for a Mon rebellion, which assumed such alarming
proportions that he had to leave Manipur and hurry southwards.
When he arrived in Rangoon, order had already been restored
by the Viceroy of Pegu, but it was whispered by the Armenians,
the inveterate enemies of the East India Company, that the
Chief of Negrais had assisted the rebels with arms. On
6 October Burmese troops, secretly assembled in the nearby
jungle, rushed the settlement and massacred its inhabitants.
Two of the English assistants, who escaped the slaughter by
hiding, were subsequently captured and brought before
Alaungpaya. He told them that he had ordered the complete
destruction of the settlement because he had received no reply
to a letter which he had sent to the king of England.

The expedition up the Chindwin, from which Alaungpaya
had been recalled in 1759, inflicted upon Manipur one of the
worst disasters in its history. Imphal was occupied, and thousands of people deported for settlement in the Sagaing and

Amarapoora districts. Among them were boatmen, silk workers
and silversmiths. From this time onwards the astrologers at the
Burmese Court were Manipuri Brahmins, while Manipuris
formed a cavalry regiment in the Burmese army known as
'Cassay Horse'.

The Mon rebellion, which gave Alaungpaya the excuse for
carrying out his threat to destroy the Negrais settlement, was
the prelude to a new series of wars with Siam. Thousands of
Mons again fled to that country, and the border became the
scene of chronic raiding and counter-raiding. This alone
would have provided an adequate *casus belli* for a monarch
unable to settle down to a peaceable existence. But the Delta
was again badly depopulated, and he hoped to colonize it by
wholesale deportations from the conquered territory. He
planned also to bring the proud state of Chiengmai to its knees.
The invasion, which began late in 1759, proceeded by way of
Tavoy down to Tenasserim, then across the hills to the Gulf of
Siam and northwards to Ayuthia. The attack from the south
took the Siamese completely by surprise; their main forces were
guarding the westward approaches.

By April 1760 Alaungpaya had encircled the city and the
siege was in full progress. The Burmese brought up heavy guns
and the king himself superintended the firing of one of the
batteries. On a day in May, while he was watching the loading
of a heavy cannon, it burst and he was so badly wounded that
the siege operations were suspended. The whole army began a
hurried retreat homewards, carrying their wounded leader with
them. At Taikkala, just before the Salween was reached, he
succumbed to his wounds. His body was borne reverently back
to his home town, Shwebo, where it was buried in the presence of great crowds of his mourning subjects. He had reigned
only eight years and was not yet forty-six at the time of his
death.

CHAPTER XI

BURMA UNDER THE EARLY
KONBAUNGSET KINGS (1760-1795)

ALAUNGPAYA founded the last Burmese dynasty, the Konbaungset line, which occupied the throne until its last king, Thibaw Min, was deposed by the British in 1885. The new vigour, infused into the Burmese people by the spectacular achievements of their great leader, was exploited by his sons Hsinbyushin and Bodawpaya with a success unparalleled in the history of the nation. They became the terror of their neighbours. They reduced Chiengmai, burnt Ayuthia to the ground, rolled back invading Chinese armies, conquered Arakan, ravaged Manipur, Kachar and Jaintia, and finally gained control over Assam. Expansion and conquest were the keynotes of Burmese policy up to 1824. But it was a foolish and extravagant policy, which took no heed of the resources of the country, and for that reason alone must ultimately have failed, even if it had not led Bagyidaw to threaten the British position in Bengal, and so precipitate the first Anglo-Burmese War (1824-26).

The short reign of Naungdawgyi (1760-63) saw no less than four rebellions. The most serious was that of Minkaung Nawrahta, who seized Ava and planned to restore the Toungoo dynasty. While besieging the city in 1760, Naungdawgyi received in audience Captain Walter Alves, who had been deputed by the Calcutta authorities to demand the punishment of the perpetrators of the Negrais massacre. The king, who was in urgent need of munitions, was therefore extremely anxious for the Company to resume trading relations. But he refused to consider any measures of reparation. Alves on the other hand had no power to negotiate any resumption of trade: his instructions were to wind up the Company's affairs in Burma. A further difficulty arose from the fact that there were still English captives in Burmese hands, and in order to secure their release, Alves had to promise to leave two of them behind

to look after the Company's property at Bassein, pending recon-
sideration of the question of withdrawal.

The decision, however, to sever all relations with Burma was
final, and during the cold season of 1761–62 Alves had to make
a further trip to Burma from Calcutta to bring away the two men
and the property he had had to leave behind on his previous
mission. Naungdawgyi raised no further difficulties, but gave
him a letter for the Governor of Bengal strongly urging the
reopening of trade. It was to no purpose; the Company had
decided that trade with Burma did not pay, and, with the
French for the time being reduced to impotence in India, there
was no fear of a revival of their influence in the land of peacocks
and pagodas.

The troubles of Naungdawgyi's reign taught his successor,
Hsinbyushin (1763–76), the old lesson that a capital in Upper
Burma must command the Kyauksè area. Shwebo was too far
away, and in 1765 he transferred his capital back to Ava. A
move to Rangoon would have been wiser, but the fear of
further Mon rebellions was an insuperable objection to such a
step. The idea never seems to have occurred to anyone that the
best cure for them would have been to foster the prosperity of
the potentially rich Delta region on a basis of sound administration. Upper Burma was the cradle of Burmese nationalism,
which was implacably hostile to any signs of Mon recovery.
Under such conditions the revival of Tabinshwehti's policy of
fusion was unthinkable.

So the barren policy of subjugating Siam was again adopted.
Exactly two centuries after Bayinnaung's conquest of Ayuthia
in 1564 the old claim to overlordship was revived by Hsinbyushin, and a fresh series of Burmese invasions began. The
initial operations brought dazzling success. In March 1767 the
city of Ayuthia was captured by the Burmese and reduced to a
heap of ruins. Thousands of captives were deported together
with vast booty. Such was the vandalism of the conquerors that
almost all the royal records were burnt. "The king of Han-
thawadi (Bayinnaung) waged war like a monarch," wrote a
Siamese chronicler, "but the king of Ava like a robber."

The destruction of Ayuthia was only the beginning of the
struggle. Out of the ashes of the old capital a new Siamese

national movement had its birth, which was to sweep the
Burmese out of the country in a remarkably short space of time.
A band of Siamese under a leader, known to Burmese history
as Paya Tak (P'ya Taksin in Siamese), cut their way out of
Ayuthia and took refuge in Cambodian territory. Within only a
few months Paya Tak was at the head of a formidable army,
which began systematically to wipe out the Burmese garrisons
and restore Siamese authority. By the end of 1768 he had
regained Ayuthia and started to build a new capital at Bangkok
nearer the sea. At the moment when Siam was thus rapidly
recovering from her defeat, Hsinbyushin was powerless to
resume the offensive; every man he could spare was needed for
the defence of his country against a determined attempt by the
Chinese to conquer it.

The Gwe Shans at Okpo and the Gwe Karens near Pegu
had been the prime movers in the great revolt of 1740. They
went on to stir up further trouble. They had joined Alaungpaya,
but their raids upon the northern Shan states had forced him
to send a punitive expedition against them in 1758–59. The
survivors took refuge in Mongmit and Hsenwi, and also in
Menglien, a trans-Salween state. From these places they began
to carry their raids across the Chinese border; and when the
widow of their original leader, Gonna-ein, stirred up Kengtung
to attack Kenghung, a dependency of China, the Yunnan
government jumped to the mistaken conclusion that the
Burmese were at the bottom of the trouble.

This suspicion was strengthened in 1764, when a Burmese
army, marching against Siam, passed through Kengtung. Indeed
the Burmese attacks on Siam had created general uneasiness;
and when in the next year a Burmese general appeared on the
Salween to collect tribute from some minor sawbwas, who were
under Chinese protection, although they had paid it to both
sides for centuries, they now complained to China. This was
the immediate cause of hostilities.

Early in 1766 the Yunnan forces invaded Kengtung. The
Burmese fearing repercussions in northern Siam, which they
still held, sent help to the sawbwa, and the Chinese were driven
out. The ignominy of this repulse caused the Viceroy of Yunnan
to commit suicide. His successor was given a free hand by the

Emperor Chien-lung to take all necessary measures to reduce Burma to submission. Little did he realize that the exploits of Alaungpaya had given the Burmese an entirely new estimation of themselves. They had become a conquering race and feared no one on earth. Hence, when the Viceroy called on the Court of Ava to submit, Hsinbyushin replied by sending an army to invade Hsenwi.

The Chinese first tried the well-known route into northern Burma. They captured Bhamo by surprise and proceeded to attack the Burmese frontier force at Kaungton. But the Kaungton stockade held until reinforcements arrived from Ava which enabled the Burmese to take the offensive and drive the Chinese back beyond Bhamo. Another Burmese army advanced to Waingmaw, south of Myitkyina, defeated a Chinese force at the Nammyin Creek and entered Chinese territory.

These perplexing reverses caused yet another change in the Yunnan government. A third Viceroy, Ming Jui, a son-in-law of the emperor, now took up the task and planned to launch a double attack on Burma, as soon as the rainy season of 1767 ended. The main Chinese army was to approach Ava through Hsenwi, Lashio and Hsipaw, and down the Namtu river. The second was to try the Bhamo route again. The attack nearly succeeded; large Burmese forces were tied up in Siam, where the situation was beginning to turn in favour of Paya Tak. Ming Jui's army, marching by the southern route followed by the Manchu force a century earlier, when chasing Yung-li, defeated two Burmese armies, and got as far as Singaung, only thirty miles from Ava (February 1768). So critical was the situation that Hsinbyushin prepared to evacuate his capital. A third Burmese force, however, marched into Hsipaw and Hsenwi and cut the Chinese communications. When Ming Jui in difficulties began to retreat, his army was surrounded and suffered disaster. A few managed to cut their way out, but the Viceroy himself, unable to extricate his main body, sent his pigtail as a present to his emperor and committed suicide. The other Chinese army, which had entered Burma by the Bhamo route, should have rescued him; but, instead of pressing on down the Irrawaddy, its commander wasted time by besieging the famous Kaungton stockade, which defied all attempts to take it. His punishment at the hands of the Imperial Government was frightful.

In the following year the Chinese made their third and last attempt to reach Ava, this time by the Bhamo route again. But again they were held by the impregnable Kaungton stockade. They themselves built a great stockaded camp at Shwenyaungbin; but the Burmese took the offensive and stormed it. That was the end of the war. The Chinese asked for terms and a treaty of peace was signed at Kaungton in 1770.

The negotiations were conducted by the Burmese commanders and the terms of the treaty were not referred to the king for sanction. He was highly annoyed when he learnt that the Chinese were to be permitted to return home alive. But it was a good peace; it promoted the restoration of trade between Burma and Yunnan, and was the prelude to a long period of happier relations. The Burmese were immeasurably proud of their achievement. It was the most glorious moment in their history, but, like all such moments was frought with danger, a danger they could not suspect.

The victorious commanders, well aware of the consequences of disregarding the royal will, led off their forces upon another raid into luckless Manipur, hoping by a fresh success to appease the king's wrath. Again fortune favoured them. They drove out the raja, placed a Burmese nominee on the throne, and deported thousands more Manipuris.

The close of the Chinese war left Hsinbyushin free once more to concentrate upon Siam. From 1770 to 1776 the struggle was relentlessly carried on, and only ceased with his death in the latter year. Paya Tak, however, was equal to the emergency. He took the Laos States, drove the Burmese out of Chiengmai and completed the unification of Siam. Again and again Burmese armies penetrated the country and overran its northern provinces; but they failed to hold them. In 1773 their Mon levies, mustered for service, mutinied, captured Martaban and chased the Burmese into Rangoon, which they burnt to the ground. Burmese reinforcements, however, drove them off, and again thousands of them fled into Siam. A Burmese force, which pursued the refugees along the Three Pagodas route, was surrounded and captured by the Siamese.

The Mon mutineers, who burnt Rangoon, destroyed also a number of ships that were being built on the stocks. The chief shipwrights were French, who had obtained royal permission to establish a shipyard there in 1768, five years after the close of the Seven Years' War. They had built some fine ships there, including one of 1500 tons, the *Lauriston*, which mounted fifty guns. The Mons made no attempt to molest them, but when the Burmese retook the place, they massacred the inhabitants. The wives of the Frenchmen were forced to stand by while their husbands, bound hand and foot, were thrown into the river. Then they themselves were sold by their captors. One was a grand-daughter of Constant Phaulkon. One Frenchman of great strength broke his bonds and swam ashore. His feat so impressed the Burmese that they let him go free.

The wars with Siam stopped temporarily during the reign of Singu, Hsinbyushin's eldest son, who reigned from 1776 to 1782. He was inefficient as a ruler, and spent his time making pilgrimages to pagodas. The common people were glad of the respite from war, but the ministers had no respect for such a king, and in 1782 a palace intrigue led to his murder. The only fighting during his reign was in Manipur, where the deposed raja made two abortive attempts to regain his throne. But the country was so thoroughly devastated that it was useless to the Burmese.

Bodawpaya, the eldest surviving son of Alaungpaya, who seized the throne in 1782, made a clean sweep of all possible rivals in the royal family. Cruelty so horrible cannot be justified, and those who attempt to do so on the ground of necessity close their eyes to the fact that his victims included many women and small children. But, though unjustifiable, the traditional massacre of Royal Kinsmen is understandable. Chaos and civil war threatened the state, and any surviving claimant might turn *minlaung*. No sooner was Bodawpaya seated on the throne than a faction, led by a brother who had escaped execution, and Maha Thihathura, one of Hsinbyushin's most distinguished commanders, plotted to overthrow him. When the plot was discovered, they, with every member of their families and all their servants, were put to death. Shortly afterwards still another aspirant to the throne entered the palace with 200 desperate men in an attempt to murder the king. They were overcome by the palace guard and slaughtered to a man. The district of Paungga near Sagaing, where they had made their plans, were treated to a bloodbath in which villages were burnt, fruit trees cut down and standing crops destroyed.

The reign, which opened so grimly, was a long one for a Burmese king; it lasted until 1819, and the note of grimness continued throughout. In September 1783 the Mons made yet another tragic attempt to free themselves from the Burmese yoke. Numbers of them from the Bassein province made a surprise attack on Rangoon and captured it. The Burmese seized all the available guns and ammunition from the European ships in the port, and forced 150 Europeans to help them against the insurgents, who were beaten, but only after heavy fighting.

As soon as order had been restored in his turbulent kingdom, Bodawpaya addressed himself to the task of administration. In 1784 he ordered a general revenue inquest. Throughout the country myothugyis and village headmen had to appear before the royal commissioners and furnish full statements regarding the boundaries of their jurisdiction, its population, products and revenue. It was the first to be carried out since Thalun's. Many of the records compiled in the course of the survey are extant today and afford first-hand historical evidence of the prevailing conditions. They show, for instance, that the total population was less than two millions.

The king's aim was, very naturally, to increase his revenue; but the record was also useful for the establishment of legal claims, and a royal decree declared that these should not lapse with a change of monarch. The precise value of this is doubtful, since no king considered himself bound by the acts of his predecessors. Nevertheless, in Bodawpaya's Burma, as in Saxon England, 'custom was the king of men', and its reduction to writing must have acted as a deterrent to the rapacity of local officials, whose tyranny could be worse than that of the monarch, so far as the ordinary people were concerned. A further inquest was held in 1803.

The most far-reaching act of the reign was the conquest of Arakan. During the long anarchy, which had prevailed since

Sandawizaya's murder in 1731, refugees had often appeared at
the Burmese Court inviting intervention. At last, one of them,
a chief named Hari, persuaded Bodawpaya that the people of
the distracted land would welcome him as their ruler. So at the
end of the year 1784 four Burmese forces invaded Arakan by
land and sea, and after some slight operations gained a complete
victory.

In February 1785 King Thamada, all the royal family and
no less than 20,000 of his people were deported to Burma.
Arakan became a provincial administration under a viceroy,
supported by a Burmese garrison. The famous Mahamuni
image, which Anawrahta had failed to bring to Burma, was the
chief item among the booty. It was housed at a shrine, the
Arakan Pagoda at Mandalay, built specially for it, and until the
end of the dynasty received daily offerings, borne with stately
ceremonial from the Palace.

When they annexed Arakan, however, the Burmese had
bitten off more than they could chew. Revolt after revolt broke
out, and as their rule became more and more repressive, with the
hateful practice of deportation as its chief remedy against
disorder, thousands of Arakanese fled over the border into the
Chittagong jungles, which belonged to the East India Company's Presidency of Bengal. Their attempts to reconquer their
country from bases in the unadministered tracts behind the
British frontier provoked a series of disputes, which in the long
run were the main cause of the first Anglo-Burmese War.

In the same year that Arakan fell, Bodawpaya organized a
great campaign for the reconquest of Siam. It was a fateful
decision, showing that like the restored Bourbons of a slightly
later date he had 'learnt nothing and forgotten nothing'. The
resumption of the futile struggle brought nothing but ex-
haustion and impoverishment to his country. He was a religious
maniac, dominated by the white elephant myth. He announced
that he was Arimittiya, the coming Buddha, and became
convinced that he was destined to be a world conqueror.

Right from the start his plans miscarried. In the first campaign (1785–86) the army he personally led over the Three
Pagodas Pass met with disaster through his own incompetence,
and he himself barely escaped capture. Even after this sorry

beginning the struggle went on for many years. It degenerated into a succession of raids and counter-raids, which depopulated the frontier Shan states, reduced parts of Siam and Tenasserim to a desert, caused a fresh Mon exodus, and led to a state of chronic dacoity over large tracts of Burma. The Siamese were still raiding Tenasserim for slaves when the British occupied the province in 1824.

As the reign proceeded and difficulties multiplied, the king's religious mania became more pronounced. He persecuted heretics and decreed the death penalty for drinking intoxicants, smoking opium and even for killing an ox or a buffalo. When the Buddhist clergy essayed to moderate some of the worst of his excesses, he announced plans to reform the Order and confiscated monastic lands. White elephant worship was carried to extremes previously unknown. It is one of the chief themes of the chronicles of his reign.

If the requisitions of men for military service caused frightful hardships to his subjects, no less did his demands for forced labour on works of Buddhist merit, particularly to the Shans, Mons and Arakanese. In particular he tried to build an enormous pagoda 500 feet in height, that was to be the wonder of the world. The unfinished monstrosity may still be seen at Mingun, not far from his capital. For seven years, 1790–97, thousands of Arakanese and other deportees worked on its construction under the personal supervision of the king, who housed his court in temporary buildings on an island in the river close by. He told Captain Hiram Cox, who visited him there, that every night the Thagyamin, king of the spirit world, sent angels to augment the work done by human labour during the day. But when the sceptical captain was taken to inspect the work, he noted the signs of candle-wax everywhere on the bricks and was quietly amused that the heavenly visitors should need the aid of artificial light for their task.

In contrast with his aggressive policy towards his neighbours, Bodawpaya scrupulously maintained good relations with China. Five times during his reign did he welcome Chinese missions at Amarapoora, his capital city. Four Burmese missions to Pekin are recorded. Prisoners of war were restored, presents and titles exchanged, and frontier friction almost

ceased. It was the first sustained effort by Burma to develop
friendly relations with a foreign power.

The Indian frontier on the other hand, like the Siamese,
became the scene of growing disorder. Bodawpaya's repeated
demands for forced labour and conscript service, and the
rapacity of his local officials, drove the Arakanese into desperate
resistance. In 1794 large-scale rebellion flared up. The rebels
were assisted by armed bands from the Chittagong district,
where thousands of refugees were settled. Against the strong
forces sent in by the Burmese the revolt collapsed as suddenly
as it had begun, and again crowds of Arakanese took refuge
inside British territory. They were pursued by a Burmese
force of 5000 men, which crossed the river Naaf and established
a base on the British side of the frontier.

To Colonel Erskine, who was despatched by Calcutta to
deal with the incident, the Governor of Arakan explained that
his orders were to capture three Arakanese chiefs, who were
rebel leaders. Erskine promised to apprehend the men, and if on
investigation the charges against them were substantiated, to
hand them over to the Burmese. This was done, and the whole
Burmese force retired across the border with their captives.

The British authorities, distinctly worried by the possible
consequences of this dangerous situation, decided that an
attempt must be made to place relations with Burma on a
proper footing. Since the days of Captain Alves and the
evacuation of the Bassein factory, official relations between
the two powers had ceased. It was felt to be all the more
necessary to cultivate friendship with Burma, since a new war
with France had just begun, and the French were, not without
cause, suspected of harbouring designs upon Burma as a
possible base for warlike designs against British India. Accordingly in 1795 Sir John Shore, the Governor-General, deputed
Captain Michael Symes as British Ambassador to the Court
of Ava.

CHAPTER XII

BRITAIN AND BURMA (1795-1826)

THE documents dealing with the despatch of Symes's mission
show clearly that the chief object of the Government of India in
seeking to re-establish relations with Burma was to prevent a
possible French move in that direction. The Arakan frontier
incident was seen mainly as a disturbing factor, which might
lead King Bodawpaya to grant the French the hospitality of his
harbours, and thus open the way for an extension of their
influence in his country. Calcutta either failed to grasp, or
deliberately shut its eyes to, the fact that the presence of thousands of Arakanese refugees in the Chittagong area constituted a
problem that must be firmly tackled, otherwise further difficulties were bound to arise, which might ruin any diplomatic
approaches to the Court of Ava.

The experience of the War of American Independence was
still fresh in Sir John Shore's mind. French activities had at one
time seriously threatened the British position in India. French
ships, built or repaired in Burmese harbours, had proved
extremely dangerous to English shipping. And though during
the war the French dockyard at Rangoon had had to be abandoned, it was known that Bussy had suggested to his home
government that Burma was the best base from which the
British in Bengal might be attacked. The Pondicherry records
contain some interesting letters written by Bussy showing that
at the end of the war there was even a plan for transferring
French establishments from India to the coast of Burma. He
went so far as to send an agent, M. Geslin, in 1783 to negotiate
a treaty with Bodawpaya. In August of the following year,
however, he reported that the scheme was impracticable, the
country was in a state of anarchy, and conquest was out of the
question. The Rangoon dockyard was never, in fact, reopened
by the French, but there were close relations between their
islands of Bourbon and Mauritius and Burmese ports.

Symes's mission in 1795 was in point of fact not the first

English effort to renew direct relations with the Court of Ava. Three years earlier Lord Cornwallis had sent a private merchant, Captain Sorrel, on a semi-official visit to Amarapoora to ask for certain concessions to British traders. The friendly reception he reported on his return encouraged Shore to hope that much might be gained by an official approach. Symes's mission, therefore, was to some extent a follow-up of Sorrel's; included in his instructions was the negotiation of a commercial treaty, with special mention of the teak trade. But his main injunctions were to seek to remove the causes of misunderstanding over the Arakan frontier incident, and to deprive the French of the use of Burmese harbours.

His reception was a strange mixture of friendly hospitality and studied rudeness. The latter, he was given to understand, was due to the unwillingness of the Court of Ava to treat on terms of equality with the representative of a subordinate government. He was twice invited to attend a general audience at court. On the first occasion the king did not put in an appearance; on the second he was present, but deliberately ignored the members of the English mission. The ministers handed Symes a list of trading concessions, in which, among other things, permission was given for an English Resident to be sent to Rangoon to facilitate intercourse between the two governments.

Symes published the account of his experiences in a delightful book, full of interesting information about the country and its history. But his report quite misled Sir John Shore, chiefly because of his rosy optimism regarding the results of his mission. Hence, when Captain Hiram Cox was sent in 1796 as British Resident and found his task impossible, because of the obstructionist tactics of the officials and the improved technique of humiliation which his firm stand evoked from the Court, Shore thought that he, and not the Burmese, was to blame, and made what amounted to an apology to Bodawpaya for his conduct.

Cox warned the Government of India that, if the Arakanese frontier question were not settled according to their wishes, the Burmese threatened to invade Bengal, and that they were actually planning intervention in Assam. The Mons, he said, looked for French aid, with which to make another attempt at independence.

Shore could not believe that this was a reliable estimate of the situation. Wellesley, on the other hand, on succeeding Shore, decided that it was, and expressed his entire satisfaction with Cox's conduct. It was felt, however, to be unwise to court further insults, and Cox's place—he returned in disgust to Calcutta early in 1798—was left vacant. The attention of the Government of India was concentrated upon Tipu of Mysore and the Indian situation.

In that same year occurred a further abortive Arakanese rising, and, in consequence, another exodus of refugees. It was estimated that there were no less than 50,000 of them in the Chittagong district. So desperate was their plight that in 1799 Cox was sent to superintend relief measures, and died there while engaged upon his difficult task.

Once again a Burmese force crossed the frontier, repulsed a military police detachment, but soon withdrew, after demanding the expulsion of all the Arakanese. When as a result of this Captain Hill was sent to discuss the situation with the Burmese Viceroy at Mrohaung, the latter refused to negotiate on any terms save total expulsion, and threatened war, if the demand was not met. Lord Wellesley, however, refused on 'grounds of humanity' to consider expulsion. Instead, he proclaimed the frontier closed to Arakanese moving in either direction, and reinforced the troops and police there. Then he commissioned Major William Francklin, an oriental scholar, to study the reports of Symes and Cox and suggest a policy.

Francklin suggested that an attempt should be made to negotiate a treaty of subsidiary alliance with Bodawpaya. Wellesley accepted the suggestion, and was about to send Francklin to carry it out, when the return of Symes from furlough in England provided him with a more suitable envoy. Symes went on this second mission provided with a magnificent escort, designed by the grandiose Wellesley to impress the Court of Ava with the full majesty of the British raj, and with a draft treaty of military aid in his portfolio.

His instructions informed him that there was reason to believe that Bodawpaya contemplated abdication, and that in

such an event the Toungoo Prince was expected to attempt to
deprive the Heir Apparent of the succession. He was therefore
to offer military support to the Heir Apparent against such a
contingency. How such a baseless rumour ever reached
Wellesley the records do not show. Symes was far too discreet
to follow up such a ludicrously irrelevant suggestion. In any
case his treatment from the moment of his arrival in Burma
made such a line of action quite out of the question. The very
magnificence of his escort challenged the Burmese to heap
every possible humiliation upon him. His patience and firmness,
however, enabled him to obtain from the ministers a verbal
disavowal of the Viceroy of Arakan's threat of war; but they
refused to consider anything short of the complete expulsion of
the refugees. Symes left the capital solemnly warning the
ministers that war might ensue.

The rebuff was not followed up by force of arms: the
Governor-General was too busily engaged with the Marathas.
The theory was therefore propounded that the Court of Ava
could not have realized how serious its conduct appeared to the
Government of India and must be given an opportunity to
apologize. So Captain Canning, who had been a member of
Symes's staff, was in 1803 deputed to Ava in the hope of
bringing the recalcitrant Court to a more reasonable frame of
mind. He got no further than Rangoon. A violently anti-
British governor made things so unpleasant for him that he had
to return to Calcutta. Notwithstanding this deliberately pro-
vocative treatment, however, there was no longer any talk of
war. For one thing Symes had reported that French influence
in Burma was negligible. The frontier also had quietened down:
the stronger guard stationed there was having a salutary effect.

For some years the Burma question receded into the background. In 1809, however, when Lord Minto, engaged upon
the elimination of French power in the East, blockaded the
islands of Mauritius and Bourbon, it was deemed necessary, in
view of their old connection with Burmese ports, to reassure
the Court of Ava regarding British policy. Again Canning was
sent. This time he was received with cordiality. The British
action had caused no alarm in Burma, he was informed, since
relations with the French islands had ceased for some years,

Travelling by the Irrawaddy to and from the capital he noted the signs of depopulation and misery, that were the result of the constant requisitions of man-power and supplies for Bodaw-paya's unsuccessful Siamese campaigns. He formed the opinion that Burmese power was so rapidly on the decline that it could no longer be considered threatening. But the spirit of bravado was as strong as ever. The Heir Apparent naively told him that his father was bent on annexing Chittagong and Eastern Bengal. In reporting this to the Governor-General, Canning urged the occupation of Arakan as a precautionary measure.

Just when the Government of India, notwithstanding this last warning was lulling itself into a false sense of security regarding the Arakan frontier, an outbreak of a far more serious nature than ever before occurred. A new leader, Chin Byan, the son of a refugee myothugyi, who had settled at Harbang, crossed the frontier in 1811 at the head of a formidable force secretly collected in British territory, took the Burmese completely by surprise and captured Mrohaung. Almost before the British were aware of what had happened, the Government at Calcutta received an urgent message from Chin Byan offering to bring Arakan under British suzerainty in return for recognition and help.

This embarrassing offer was at once rejected, and Captain Canning was sent on yet another mission to Burma. The Court of Ava refused to listen to any explanation: they were convinced that only with British aid could Chin Byan have assembled and led such an expedition. To make matters worse, while Canning was assuring the ministers that if Chin Byan were defeated, the British would take effective steps to prevent the rebels from again taking refuge in Chittagong, the very thing that he promised should not happen, did happen; the rebels were driven out and returned to British territory as easily as they had left it. The small British frontier force failed to make any contact with them. They disappeared into the trackless jungles of the unadministered territory.

The Burmese sent parties over the frontier in search of Chin Byan. The Viceroy of Arakan threatened to invade Chittagong with 80,000 men, if the rebel leaders were not handed over. It was bluff: the actual force under his command

was less than a tenth of that number, and, as soon as the wet
monsoon began, had to be withdrawn to Mrohaung. But the
Calcutta authorities were quite helpless to cope with the new
situation. Every dry season during the next few years 'King-
bering', as he was known to the British, broke out of his hiding-
place and raided Arakan, only to be driven out by the Burmese,
who repeatedly crossed the frontier in vain endeavours to take
him. Attempts by the British to co-operate with the Burmese
against the elusive rebel leader failed, and neither side alone
could catch him.

The game of hide-and-seek went on until early in 1815.
Then, as unexpectedly as they had started, the rebel raids
ceased, and it was discovered that Chin Byan was dead.
Although this embarrassing incident had ended, irreparable
harm had been done to Anglo-Burmese relations. The Burmese
had been led grossly to underestimate British power. They
failed to realize that the Indian situation was the real cause of
the weakness shown in the Chittagong area, and that, until the
Marathas were decisively defeated, the Government of India
was not in a position to take a strong line on its eastern frontier.

Before the Maratha war ended the Burmese threat was to
take on a new shape. The first warning that the Burmese
contemplated intervention in Assam had been given by
Captain Cox. The country had long been in a state of chaos.
As far back as 1792 Captain Welch, sent there by Lord Cornwallis, had reported that only complete annexation would
restore order; but non-intervention was then the ruling policy.
In 1817 the Burmese invaded and placed their nominee on the
throne. He was soon overthrown. In 1819 they returned and
placed another raja on the throne. He also was driven out and
fled to British territory. This time the Burmese returned to
stay. So a situation developed very similar to the one which had
obtained on the Arakan frontier. Assamese leaders recruited
and collected arms in British territory, and made futile attempts
to free their country from the Burmese.

In 1819 Bagyidaw, Bodawpaya's grandson, succeeded to
the throne of Burma. He appointed the brilliant and ambitious
general, Bandula, as governor of Assam, and it soon became
evident that an aggressive move against Bengal was being

planned. The Burmese drove out the raja of Manipur and chased him into Cachar. The raja of Cachar fled to British territory, and the Government of India, fearing an attack on Eastern Bengal, declared a protectorate over his state, and sent in a force which compelled the Burmese to withdraw. That was in 1824.

Meanwhile troubles had again broken out on the Arakan frontier. In 1823 the Burmese seized Shapuri Island on the British side of the estuary of the Naaf. A British force reoccupied it, but an attempt to set up an Anglo-Burmese frontier commission failed. Then in January 1824 Bandula took over the command in Arakan and began to concentrate troops for a march on Chittagong.

War could no longer be avoided. The East India Company had its hands free in India. Bandula and Bagyidaw had chosen a singularly inappropriate moment at which to challenge it. Neither had the slightest idea of its real strength. It came as a complete surprise to them that the British could treat Arakan and Assam as of slight strategic importance and concentrate upon a large-scale sea-borne invasion of Lower Burma from an assembly point in the Andaman Islands. Hence, when the fleet and its convoy of transports passed up the river on 10 May, 1824, the British achieved a complete strategic surprise. They captured Rangoon without a blow.

The war which followed has been called the worst-managed one in British military history. No one could quarrel with the main plan of campaign, which was to capture Rangoon and advance up the Irrawaddy to the capital, while at the same time conducting subsidiary operations for the occupation of Assam, Arakan and the Tenasserim coast. But Sir Archibald Campbell's expeditionary force was so badly supplied with transport that it was tied down to Rangoon, unable to press through to Ava before the wet monsoon rendered a campaign up the Irrawaddy impossible. It had been erroneously assumed that the Mons of the Delta would gladly provide the necessary transport, and plentiful supplies of fresh food as well. It was even fondly hoped that the loss of Rangoon would cause Bagyidaw to sue for peace.

So the invaders were held up for six months during the rainy season at Rangoon, and it was not long before only a few hundreds of the original force of 11,000 were fit for operations, such was the havoc wrought by fever and dysentery. It has been estimated that during the first year while battle casualties accounted for a death-roll of only 3.5 per cent, no less than 45 per cent of the troops died of disease, and the chief victims were the Europeans.

The Burmese army under Bandula began operations by crossing the Naaf and routing a small detachment of Company's troops. The news of the British capture of Rangoon, however, put a stop to this campaign. Two successive generals, the Thonba Wungyi and the Kyi Wungyi, failed to retake the city, and Bandula had to be recalled and directed south to drive the invaders into the sea. Such indeed was his expectation as he marched on Rangoon with 60,000 men and a considerable artillery train. His two main attacks, delivered early in December 1824, were so severely repulsed that his army began to disintegrate and he was forced to beat a hasty retreat with 7000 picked troops to Danubyu. Rapid arrivals of reinforcements enabled Sir Archibald Campbell to organize a field force with Prome as its objective. On 1 April, 1825, while attempting to hold Danubyu, Bandula was killed in action. His whole army thereupon retired in disorder, leaving the British to push on unhampered to Prome, where they went into cantonments in preparation for the next rainy season.

While these operations were in progress, two other campaigns began with the Burmese capital as their ultimate objective. Early in 1825 Mrohaung was taken and soon afterwards Cheduba and Sandoway occupied. But it was found impracticable to transport an army across the Arakan Yoma, and the further plan had to be abandoned. In the north the Burmese were driven from Cachar, which they had again invaded, and it was hoped to follow them up through Manipur. But the mountainous country and torrential rains forced the abandonment of this campaign also. Later on the exiled raja, Gambhir Singh, assisted by British officers, systematically freed his country, but the plan of an expedition was given up. There were also operations in Assam, which cleared the Burmese out of that country, and presented the British with many new problems of frontier administration.

Bandula's death and the British occupation of Prome caused

panic at the Burmese capital. In order to gain time to raise fresh armies an armistice was proposed, and in October 1825 the Kyi Wungyi met Sir Archibald Campbell twenty-five miles north of Prome for peace talks. The discovery that the Burmese were preparing to attack Prome brought these to a summary conclusion, and fighting was resumed. This was the last serious Burmese stand. After its defeat progress by both land and river was rapid.

At Malun peace talks were again started by the Kyi Wungyi, but the British peace terms, which comprised the cession of Arakan, Tenasserim, Assam and Manipur and the payment of an indemnity in rupees equal to a million sterling, so staggered the Burmese that the discussions were broken off. Not until the British army was at Yandabo within a few days' march of the capital did the Burmese finally give way, after many attempts to haggle over the terms as the expeditionary force made its way through Upper Burma, brushing aside such enemy forces as were from time to time flung against it. On 24 February, 1826, the Treaty of Yandabo was ratified and the British advanced no farther.

By the cession of Arakan and Tenasserim Burma lost most of her sea frontage though retaining the ports of Rangoon, Martaban and Bassein. The safety of the North-East Frontier of India was assured by the cession of Assam and the undertaking by the Court of Ava to abstain from interference in Manipur, Cachar and Jaintia. Among additional stipulations it was laid down that an indemnity of a crore of rupees was to be paid by instalments, a British Resident was to be entertained at Ava and a Burmese Ambassador at Calcutta, while a separate treaty of commerce was to be negotiated.

The war, which, had it been properly organized, should have lasted only a matter of months, had gone on for nearly two years and cost thirteen millions sterling. The total forces employed by the British ran to 40,000 men, of whom no less than 15,000 lost their lives, though only four per cent were battle deaths. But the course of Burmese history had now been radically altered. The British had gained possession of two large provinces of the Empire of Ava, and must either ultimately relinquish them, or go on until they occupied the whole country. For some years the main question at issue was whether they were worth keeping.

CHAPTER XIII

THE FIRST RESIDENCY AND
THE ANNEXATION OF PEGU (1826–1855)

THE old aggressive Burma was now no more. The military power, which had carried terror from Ayuthia to Mrohaung, defeated Chinese armies and made and unmade rajas in Assam and Manipur, had been irreparably shattered. The dynasty of Alaungpaya never recovered from the shock. King Bagyidaw, whom as a boy at his grandfather's palace Captain Hiram Cox portrayed as a charming personality, became subject to recurring fits of melancholia, which ultimately led to insanity. Their best harbours, Rangoon, Martaban and Bassein, were still in Burmese hands, but the Court of Ava, nursing a grievance against the British, who had so rudely robbed it of prestige as well as territory, became still more remote and self-absorbed; and, as a result, still more unrealistic in its attitude towards the outside world. Even in the matter of its reception of British envoys it became more rather than less punctilious in its insistence upon humiliating procedure. Worse still, no attempt was made to reform the administrative and economic methods, which had contributed to the disaster.

Burmese policy during the years leading up to the war had placed the British Indian Government in a most embarrassing position. Calcutta had twice been in a state of panic over incidents occurring on the Arakan frontier. The Company had tried to avoid war by direct diplomatic intercourse, but this had broken down. In 1826 it was more than ever convinced that peace could be established only on a basis of direct relations; hence the stipulation in the treaty that a British Resident must be entertained in Ava and a Burmese Ambassador deputed to Calcutta.

Unfortunately there was some delay in appointing a British Resident. He should have been placed on a proper footing before the army retired from Yandabo. But when John Crawfurd, the first Resident, arrived in the capital in September

1826, the British army was back in Rangoon, and the Court of Ava had begun to recover from its first fright. He had therefore to encounter all the arts of subterfuge, evasion and studied rudeness, with which earlier envoys had had to contend.

Crawfurd came from Singapore, where he had succeeded Raffles, and had behind him a fine record of service in Java, Siam and Malaya. Like Raffles he was a distinguished orientalist, anxious to learn all he could about the country and people he was visiting for the first time. His principal task was to negotiate the commercial treaty and to report upon the feasibility of establishing a permanent Residency. In both matters he was bitterly disappointed. The ministers did little except haggle over the outstanding instalments of the indemnity and the political clauses in the peace treaty. They whittled down his commercial proposals to such an extent that the treaty he finally obtained was almost worthless. When he left in disgust, after a stay of only a few months, he reported that it was inexpedient to appoint a permanent Resident. His *Journal of an Embassy to the Court of Ava in the Year 1827*, in which he described his experiences, takes its place with the works of Symes and Yule as one of the best accounts of the old Burmese kingdom in the English language.

At first the Supreme Government at Calcutta was convinced by his argument that a Resident no less than 1200 miles distant by water from Calcutta would occupy a position 'little better than honourable confinement'. Subsequent events, however, forced it to alter its view and appoint one. In the first place, when a duly accredited Burmese mission appeared in Calcutta and raised questions concerning the unpaid half of the indemnity and the frontiers of Arakan and Manipur, it was found to have no power to settle the points at issue, but must refer everything back to Ava. In the second place, a sharp difference of opinion occurred on the spot between the British and Burmese commissioners appointed to demarcate the boundary between Burma and Manipur. There were also disorderly incidents on the Tenasserim boundary.

To deal with this perplexing situation Major Henry Burney, the son of Fanny Burney's half-brother Richard, who had been

Second Master at the Calcutta Military Orphanage School, was appointed Resident at Ava, and arrived there in April 1830. After some initial difficulty, Burney achieved greater success personally with the Burmese than any previous British envoy. He had a charming personality, which the king himself found so attractive that he conferred the rank of Wundauk upon him, and often summoned him to the palace for heart-to-heart talks. At his best Bagyidaw was a generous-minded man, and before his mental disorder incapacitated him, his relations with the Resident were so good that many difficulties were adjusted to the satisfaction of both sides.

Burney's greatest success was in the matter of the Manipur boundary dispute. Both Manipur and Burma claimed the Kabaw Valley between the Manipur mountains and the river Chindwin. The Government of India supported the Manipur claim, but Burney from a study of Burmese records came to the conclusion that the Burmese claim was well founded, and in 1833 he managed to persuade the Supreme Government to agree to the retrocession of the valley, though it had been occupied by the Manipuris since the end of the war.

One of the most important questions at issue during the early years of the Residency was the future of the Tenasserim provinces. They proved a financial liability to the East India Company, and Burney was instructed to sound the Court of Ava regarding the question of their retrocession—at a price. The Burmese, however, were in no mood to offer reasonable terms: they mistakenly supposed that the British were so anxious to get rid of the provinces that in the end they would recover them on their own terms. Burney tried to disabuse them by suggesting that the Siamese might be willing to strike a bargain with the Company for them; but although shaken, the ministers remained intractable, and the negotiations were dropped. He also failed to persuade them to appoint a resident ambassador at Calcutta. Such a thing had never happened in Burmese history. One also suspects that it was beneath the dignity of Ava to send a resident ambassador to a mere viceroy.

From before the end of 1831 Bagyidaw had become subject to recurrent periods of insanity. During these the Chief Queen and her brother, the Minthagyi, both of low origin, controlled the Government. This was much to the distaste of a party led by the King's younger brother, Tharrawaddy Min, who was anxious to seize power and wipe out the disgrace of the Treaty of Yandabo. In 1837 Tharrawaddy carried through a successful *coup d'état* and deposed his brother.

Much against his conception of his position as Resident, Burney was forced to play an important role in the negotiations for the surrender of the capital. Both sides looked to him as the only one able to prevent the usual horrors attendant upon a palace revolution. Tharrawaddy promised that there should be no bloodshed. He broke his promise, but Burney's protests were so strong, after five ex-ministers had been done to death, that the executions stopped. No less than 200 people had lost their lives when Bagyidaw had succeeded to the throne in 1819. But Tharrawaddy could not forgive Burney for his interference. Burney, therefore, whose health had broken down under the strain of his position, relinquished his post and returned to India. He warned the Government of India that it would be unwise to appoint a successor to reside at Amarapoora, since there was considerable risk of an outrage which might endanger peace. The new king, he said, was under the influence of 'coarse ill-informed characters', who openly looked forward to the time when it might be possible to recover by force the territory lost at Yandabo.

Lord Auckland, however, did not agree with Burney, and for two more years, until July 1839, a Resident was retained, Colonel Benson, who told the Government of India that he had to live under such conditions 'as no English gentleman or more extensively no British subject ought to be exposed to'. He also left on the plea of ill-health, handing over charge to his assistant, Captain William McLeod. The latter, finding it quite impossible to live in quarters that were flooded to a depth of several feet during the wet monsoon, retired to Rangoon, from whence he was withdrawn in 1840. Thus ended the first attempt to maintain a British Residency at the Court of Ava. Tharrawaddy's joy was unbounded; the breakdown of every Resident's health at Amarapoora became his stock joke.

The severance of diplomatic relations, however, made a further war inevitable. Tharrawaddy was playing with fire. He openly proclaimed his repudiation of the Treaty of Yandabo. Wild rumours of a Burmese plan to attack Tenasserim were fanned by a significant outbreak of dacoity in the Salween neighbourhood, and even more so by a royal visit to Rangoon in October 1841 which was of the nature of a military demonstration. Nothing came of these incidents: Tharrawaddy was shrewd enough not to push things too far. But he also began to show symptoms of insanity. It started with fits of ungovernable rage, during which he might indulge in shocking cruelties. At last his conduct became so dangerous that in 1845 his sons put him under restraint. He died in the following year and was succeeded by his eldest son, Pagan Min.

It was a clear case of 'from the frying-pan into the fire'. The new king began, as was usual, by murdering a large number of his relatives. But the bloodbath did not end there: during his first two years there are said to have been no less than 6000 executions. He rarely attended to business, and local officers could do much as they pleased, so long as the due amount of revenue found its way into the Treasury. How long he would have remained on the throne, had he not drifted into war with the British, it is impossible to say.

The Second Burmese War arose out of a series of incidents apparently so trivial, that Richard Cobden in England made a slashing attack on the Governor-General of India, Lord Dalhousie, for his conduct of the negotiations leading up to it. For some years after the withdrawal of the Residency, Calcutta was plagued with complaints about ill-treatment by Burmese officials made by British subjects resident in or trading to Rangoon. Some of them were palpably frivolous, others exaggerated. In Lord Dalhousie's early days as Governor-General, while his main attention was directed to settling accounts with the Sikhs, little heed could be paid to complaints from Rangoon. But the time came when his hands were free: and it was his opinion that British prestige in the East demanded that the Burma nettle should be firmly grasped.

In 1851, Maung Ok, the Governor of Pegu Province, and no lover of the British, plainly overstepped the mark by arresting two respectable British sea captains on frivolous charges of murder, in order to extort from them and their crews a large

sum of money. Their claims for damages—somewhat excessive
in point of fact—were submitted to the Government of India,
and Dalhousie decided to demand reparation in such a way as
would render it impossible, in his judgement, for the Burmese
to refuse. Accordingly he sent Commodore Lambert in
H.M.S. *Fox*, accompanied by two Company's vessels, the
Proserpine and the *Tenasserim*, to Rangoon, with a peremptory
request for compensation and the removal of Maung Ok.

The Court of Ava promised redress and recalled the
offending Governor. But the new man, appointed in his place,
arrived with a strong body of troops, while at the same time
the garrisons at Martaban and Bassein were also heavily
reinforced. It was later discovered that he belonged to a party
at the capital which favoured an uncompromising attitude,
since it believed that the Burmese army was capable of standing
up to a British invasion. Unfortunately Lambert was the
wrong man to deal with such a situation, if a peaceable solution
was to be sought. When the Governor in a grossly insulting
manner refused to receive a deputation of British officers, who
waited on him to discuss the quite reasonable claim for damages,
with which they had been entrusted, Lambert declared a
blockade of the port of Rangoon, and proceeded to take reprisals
on Burmese shipping. A few shots were fired by the Burmese
shore batteries, which were immediately silenced by a broad-
side from the *Fox*. Then, having destroyed every Burmese
war boat within reach, the 'combustible commodore', as
Dalhousie called him in a private letter, sailed back to Calcutta.

Dalhousie at once prepared for war. He followed up
Lambert's mission by despatching a strong force bearing an
ultimatum together with a new demand for compensation, this
time to the tune of ten lakhs of rupees, to cover the cost of his
military preparations. He still hoped against hope that the
threat would cause the Court of Ava to climb down; but on
1 April, 1852, the ultimatum expired without any response
from the Burmese. A few days later the British forces occupied
Rangoon and Martaban, and the war began.

In his pamphlet *How Wars are got up in India: the Origin of
the Burmese War*, Cobden particularly censured the despatch
of a commodore of the Royal Navy to negotiate, and the

subsequent raising of the demand for compensation from a sum
equivalent to £1000 to a hundred times that amount. Actually
Dalhousie disapproved and censured Lambert's action. "If I
had the gift of prophecy I would not have employed Lambert
to negotiate," he wrote afterwards. But he was convinced that
any show of weakness, which allowed Burmese insolence a
further triumph, would endanger Britain's whole position in
the East. His answer to Cobden's criticism was that Lambert
was not the cause of the war. War had long been inevitable;
hence the actual occasion of it was comparatively unimportant.

Dalhousie was determined to avoid the mistakes of the first
war. He tackled the problems of organization, transport and
co-operation with truly masterly zeal. The measures he took
for safeguarding the health of the expeditionary force were so
effective that the mortality from disease was actually lower than
the peace-time average for the army in India. The chief
difficulty lay in the personality of the Commander-in-Chief,
General Godwin, a septuagenarian, who heartily disliked
having to co-operate with the Royal Navy, and after the death
of Rear-Admiral Austen, Jane's brother, early in the operations, bitterly complained that he, a general, should be
dependent on Austen's successor, Lambert, a mere commodore. He disagreed with Dalhousie's whole plan of campaign,
and believed, as Dalhousie put it, that nothing that was not
done in the first war could be done in the second.

The initial plan of campaign was simple; it was to seize the
three ports of Rangoon, Martaban and Bassein before the
monsoon rains began, and then await overtures from Ava.
There was originally no plan to annex more territory. The war
started as a military demonstration to force Pagan Min to
climb down and come to terms. But after taking the three ports,
Dalhousie found that he had again miscalculated in his estimation of Burmese reactions. As the rains dragged on their weary
course, no sign came from the Golden Fleet. Burmese policy
was to play a waiting game in the hope that disease would so
decimate the invaders that they would have to withdraw.

In July 1852 Dalhousie went personally to Rangoon to
confer with Godwin and Lambert. Godwin's proposal was to
push on to Amarapoora, and he was supported by the London

press, which demanded a dictated peace at the capital. Dalhousie, however, decided that the only prudent course was to annex the province of Pegu by advancing to a line somewhere north of Prome. An advance to the capital would be useless unless the annexation of the whole country were contemplated, and this was out of the question on both military and economic grounds. On the other hand the acquisition of the old kingdom of Pegu, linking up Arakan and Tenasserim, would, he thought, strengthen the British position in Burma and reduce the Court of Ava to impotence.

This proposal was conveyed to the Home Government in a brilliantly reasoned minute, which secured its assent, subject to the Court of Ava being forced to acknowledge the annexation in a treaty. When, in November, the reply arrived, Prome had just been taken, and the main Burmese army under the incompetent son of the great Bandula defeated after a mere token resistance. Dalhousie refused to tie up his plans to a treaty. He did not believe that a king of Burma would ever again consent to one, unless forced to by a march on his capital; and he had already ruled that out. He informed the Home Government that he would go ahead with the systematic occupation of the province, and as soon as that was complete, would announce its annexation by proclamation. Accordingly on 20 December, 1852, the proclamation was read with due ceremony at Rangoon, and the British province of Pegu came into being with Major Arthur Purves Phayre as its first Commissioner.

The British advance to Prome had precipitated a revolution in Amarapoora. The Mindon Prince, half-brother to the King, and leader of a party which had been opposed to the war from the start, fled in December from the capital and civil war began. In the following February the Wungyis of the Hlutdaw, wearied with Pagan Min's incompetence, deposed him and invited Mindon to become king. The new king, a sincere Buddhist who hated bloodshed, and a patriot with a high sense of public duty, signalized his accession by releasing all the Europeans imprisoned at the capital, and sending two of them, the Italian priests, Father Domingo Tarolly and Father Abbona, to meet the British Commander-in-Chief and inform him that envoys would be sent as soon as possible to discuss peace.

H

They contacted him not at Prome, as they had expected, but fifty miles higher up the river at Myede. The British had found Prome too unhealthy for use as a cantonment, and having waited there in vain for some word from Pagan Min, had decided to occupy a further slice of Burmese territory, which would give them not only a better frontier station, but also a rich belt of teak-bearing forest land. The additional territory also included in its eastern section the old city of Toungoo on the Sittang. From Myede therefore the two priests were sent back to Mindon with the news that the British had annexed the southern part of his kingdom up to a line running directly east-west across the country from Arakan to the borders of Karenni and slightly north of Myede and Toungoo. He was invited to recognize a *fait accompli.*

Arthur Phayre, who as Commissioner of Pegu was nominated by Dalhousie to negotiate with the Court of Ava, had already seen much service in Tenasserim and Arakan. At the time of his appointment to Pegu he was Commissioner of Arakan, and had won a great reputation for 'turning the swamps of Arakan into the granary of the Bay'.[1] Less known then were his pioneer researches into Arakanese chronicles and coins. Later he was to make a scholarly study of Burmese history, which resulted in the publication of the first authoritative History of Burma in the English language.[2] It was largely because of his intimate knowledge of the people and their language that Dalhousie had promoted him over the head of his senior, the Commissioner of Tenasserim, Lieutenant-Colonel Archibald Bogle, who had unwisely boasted of his ability to carry on his duties without any knowledge of the Burmese language.

Mindon Min could not believe that the British seriously intended to keep Pegu. At the end of March 1853 the Burmese peace delegation, headed by the Magwe Mingyi, the senior minister of the Hlutdaw, met the British commissioners and begged them not to insist on annexation. As a forlorn hope Dalhousie authorized Phayre to offer to give up the additional territory north of Prome in return for a treaty of peace recog-

---

[1] Laurie, W. F. B., *Sketches of D stinguished Anglo-Indians*, 1887, p. 136.
[2] Phayre, A. P., *History of Burma*, London, 1883.

nizing the British possession of Pegu. But it was useless: Mindon would never give his assent to a treaty ceding Burmese territory to a foreign power. So the negotiations were broken off, the Myede boundary was retained, and Phayre was faced with the double task of organizing a new province while at the same time seeking to establish a workable *modus vivendi* with the Court of Ava.

It was a strange and dangerous situation which faced the British when peace talks were broken off in May 1853. The Burmese, with memories of the first war in their minds, fully expected a further British advance up the Irrawaddy as soon as the wet monsoon ended. On the British side of the frontier the wildest rumours circulated of impending Burmese attacks. It was common knowledge that Mindon's brother, Kanoung Min, the Heir Apparent, was at the head of a war party, and it remained still to be seen whether Mindon could maintain himself on the throne. It was essential, therefore, that the British should make no false move. The annexed territory also was seething with rebellion. Local myothugyis at the head of guerrilla bands were the leaders of a stubborn resistance movement, which seriously hindered attempts to establish settled administration, while from across the border Burmese officials raided frontier villages.

It took three years to 'pacify' the province. The most daring of the leaders, Myat Tun, earned Dalhousie's ungrudging respect. In a private letter to Phayre he wrote:

"A man who has 4000 men under him, who repulses three British attacks, and after a very stout defence is finally routed only by a Brigadier-General, after a month's operations and with severe loss to us, must be regarded as a chief and a Soldier—and a good one too."

Only positive action from both sides could prevent a drift back into war. Fortunately both Mindon and Phayre were wise and courageous enough to take such action. Mindon set the ball rolling by a letter to Phayre assuring him of his peaceful intentions and notifying him that orders had been sent to all frontier officers to prohibit any further attacks upon the

British. Dalhousie's immediate response was to issue an official
declaration of the termination of hostilities. Then, after con-
sultation with Phayre, he decided to break the diplomatic
impasse by the appointment of an intelligence officer at the
Burmese capital. He must be a private news-agent, not in any
sense a representative of the British Government, and the king
must be fully aware of his position and duties.

Given the right man it was a brilliant idea. After some delay
the right man was discovered in the person of a Scottish piece-
goods merchant, Thomas Spears, long resident at Amarapoora,
married to a Burmese lady, and personally liked by Mindon
himself. His task was simply to keep Phayre informed by regular correspondence of the situation at the capital; but Mindon
was so delighted by his appointment that he constantly sought
to use Spears as his official channel of communication with the
British. Spears served both sides honestly and well. Both
Phayre and Mindon came to rely absolutely upon his good
judgement and common sense; and although the wary
Dalhousie often warned Phayre that Spears was simply and
solely a news-writer without any official standing, all the intercourse between Mindon and the British up to 1861 was conducted through his capable hands. Gradually frontier peace
was established and friendly relations promoted between
Rangoon and Ava.

The first striking result of this new arrangement was the
despatch of a Burmese mission of friendship led by the Dalla
Wun to Calcutta. Personally conducted by Phayre, and carried
on board the Company's steamship *Zenobia* with the national
flag of Burma at her masthead, the envoys were accorded a royal
reception by Lord Dalhousie. And although, after a round of
entertainment and sightseeing, which they much enjoyed, they
failed to persuade the Governor-General to consider the
retrocession of the lost province of Pegu, the report they took
back to Mindon of their courteous treatment so impressed him
that he at once invited the Government of India to depute a
return mission to his capital.

Thus it came about that Phayre was deputed in 1855 to
head the British mission to the Court of Ava, which is the
subject of Sir Henry Yule's delightful volume published four

years later.[1] For the first time in the long unhappy history of British diplomatic relations with Ava a British envoy was received by a Burmese king with the charming hospitality and friendliness that is so natural to the Burman, notwithstanding, in those days, his innate suspicion of the foreigner. The chief credit for this must go to Mindon personally. In these early years he cherished the quixotic hope that if only the British could be brought to realize how true a friend he could be, they would voluntarily surrender Pegu.

In one sense the mission was a failure. In spite of long private talks with the king, Phayre was unable to persuade him to sign even a general treaty of peace, making no allusion whatever to the loss of territory. But Lord Dalhousie expressed himself fully satisfied with the results of the mission.

"From its first entrance into Burmese waters until its return to our frontier" [he wrote], "the Mission was treated with the highest distinction and with the utmost hospitality and liberality . . . and I desire to record my firm conviction that peace with Burma is to the full as secure as any written treaty could have made it."

His estimate was a true one. It has only to be recalled that the Crimean War was in progress when this *entente* was developing. The Armenian community at Amarapoora was at the time busily engaged in spreading rumours that English rule in India was 'finished' and that a great Russian invasion of India was about to be launched. But neither then nor later, when the British were seriously embarrassed by the Indian Mutiny, did Mindon Min attempt to make profit out of the situation. "We do not strike a friend when he is in distress," he is reported to have replied to the advisers, who urged him to invade Pegu, when it was learnt that the British garrison there was depleted through having to send reinforcements to India. That reply is the measure not only of Mindon's statesmanship, but also of the understanding and good sense shown by Arthur Phayre and Thomas Spears in their handling of a very delicate situation.

[1] Yule, Sir H. *A Narrative of the Mission sent by the Governor-General of India to the Court of Ava in* 1855, London, 1858.

CHAPTER XIV

THE SECOND RESIDENCY AND THE ANNEXATION OF UPPER BURMA

PHAYRE served in Burma until 1867. In 1862, when the province of British Burma was formed by the amalgamation of the three divisions of Pegu, Arakan and Tenasserim, he became its first High Commissioner. As such he made two more visits to the Burmese capital, which Mindon Min transferred to Mandalay in 1860. The chief aim of British policy in these later years was to improve trading relations with Upper Burma, with the further object of developing trade with Western China, particularly along the Old Burma Road running from Bhamo into Yunnan.

The moving spirit behind this scheme was Dr. Clement Williams, who, while serving in Pegu as Assistant-Surgeon in Her Majesty's 68th Regiment, spent a furlough in Mandalay in 1860–61 and managed to get on friendly terms with the king. Hence, when in 1862 Phayre concluded a commercial treaty with Mindon, providing, among other things, for the reopening of the British Residency, Williams was the obvious man to become the first British Agent at Mandalay.

Phayre's treaty of 1862 guaranteed reciprocal rights to the subjects of both powers to trade along the Irrawaddy river and purchase whatever they required. There was to be free trade on both sides of the frontier. In conformity with this agreement the British in 1863 abolished all customs on goods entering their territory from Upper Burma, and allowed rice to be imported into Upper Burma duty free. The Burmese, however, indefinitely delayed performance of their part of the agreement. The main cause of this failure was the system of royal monopolies, which Mindon had extended to all important articles of commerce, and by which all purchases had to be made through royal brokers.

Williams concentrated his attention upon the exploration of trade routes into China. Soon after his arrival in Mandalay as

Resident, he persuaded Mindon to allow him to survey the river route to Bhamo, and, as a result of inquiries he was able to make during his stay at Bhamo, he became an enthusiast for schemes for overland trade with China.

British interest in the Old Burma Road had originally been stimulated by the Dutchman Spar's visit to London in 1683, when he almost succeeded in stirring the East India Company to approach the King of Burma for permission to plant a trading station at Bhamo. The matter was then lost sight of until Symes, in reporting on his first mission to Ava, mentioned that Burma carried on an extensive cotton trade with Yunnan. Cox, who followed him, wrote a fairly detailed report on the subject, which saw the light of day in a selection of papers on Burma published by Major Francklin in 1811.

Crawfurd in 1827 estimated the annual value of Burmese exports to China at £228,000. This so much interested the British authorities at Moulmein that they began to consider the feasibility of a route from that town to Yunnan. Captain Sprye in 1831 suggested the Salween route *via* Kianghung, and six years later Captain McLeod actually made the journey by this route with six elephants. Another doughty prospector was Dr. Richardson, who made several expeditions, the first of which took him from Moulmein to Chiengmai in 1834.

Attempts were also made to discover the ancient land route known to have once existed between China and India, and in 1835 Captain Hannay actually made the overland journey from Bengal to Bhamo. These gallant efforts had no immediate result other than the production of a number of interesting reports. In 1855, while on his first visit to Mindon Min, Phayre raised the question of the opening of the Bhamo route with China, and Yule developed the subject in his book. But the Court of Ava was strongly opposed to any plan which might tempt the British to further interference.

In 1860 the Manchester Chamber of Commerce, on the look-out for further markets for Lancashire cotton goods, petitioned the British Government to go ahead with the development of the Moulmein-Yunnan route. Their pressure was one of the causes of Phayre's visit to Mandalay in 1862 and of Dr. Clement Williams's trip to Bhamo in 1863. He

reported against the Moulmein route and strove to direct
attention to the Bhamo one. At the time, however, owing to the
Panthay revolt, which closed Yunnan to Burmese trade from
1855 to 1873, the difficulties were much greater than he
suspected. In Burma also there were serious political troubles,
which in 1866 led to the murder of the Heir Apparent. Hence,
when Phayre went again to Mandalay in that year to negotiate a
further trade agreement, the disturbed state of the country was
used as a decisive argument against all his proposals.

In the following year, when Phayre retired, he was
succeeded by Colonel Albert Fytche, a descendant of the
Elizabethan Ralph Fitch, a cousin of Tennyson the poet-
laureate, and one who, like his predecessor, had spent nearly
all his active career in Burma. He at once went to Mandalay to
negotiate a new treaty. By this time Mindon Min had changed
his mind; he needed steamers and arms to guard against
further trouble, and was willing to discuss terms.

Fytche, who was accompanied by his wife, was accorded a
most friendly reception, and returned with what was on paper
a valuable set of concessions. The king promised to abandon all
monopolies, save those on rubies, earth-oil and timber, and to
reduce Burmese customs duties to five per cent *ad valorem*. He
also granted certain rights of extra-territoriality, whereby the
Resident was invested with full jurisdiction in civil cases
between British subjects at the capital, while those between
British subjects and Burmese subjects were to be decided by a
mixed court composed of the Resident and a Burmese officer of
high rank. In addition, British agents were to sit as observers in
Burmese customs houses, and Burmese agents in British
customs houses.

In the conversations leading up to the treaty, the king agreed
to admit a resident British Agent at Bhamo, sanctioned British
exploring expeditions from Bhamo into western China, and
gave permission for British steamers to navigate the Irrawaddy
up to and beyond Mandalay. In British eyes these concessions
were far more important than the terms of the treaty itself.
Little was expected from trade with Upper Burma; the real
objective was China. It was a period of tremendous activity on
the part of the three powers specially interested in Far Eastern

expansion, Britain, France and the United States. The Suez
Canal was nearing completion, as also was the first American
trans-continental railway. Both were opened to traffic in 1869.

Britain and the United States were keenly competing for
the trade of China, concerning which somewhat exaggerated
views were current. The British, therefore, were anxiously
probing for a shorter way to the Middle Kingdom, which, it
was hoped, would give them the advantage over their com-
petitors. The French also were eagerly in the field. Henri
Mouhot had discovered the majestic ruins of Angkor in 1860.
Three years later the French proclaimed a protectorate over
the old kingdom of Cambodia, and Doudart de Lagrée at once
proposed to explore the Mekong, which he described as 'the
traditional commercial route between China and the Khmer
Empire'. In 1866 he and Francis Garnier, then an intense
anglophobe, who called Britain a 'colossus with feet of clay',
started on a journey, which took them up to Yunnan, and led to
the French decision to make themselves masters of Tongking,
'the key to China'.

Fytche's visit to Mandalay was speedily followed up by the
planting of a British agent, Captain Strover, at Bhamo in
November 1868. Before his arrival, however, the Political
Agent at Mandalay, Major E. B. Sladen, partly financed by the
Rangoon Chamber of Commerce, had made his way *via*
Bhamo to Momein (Tengyueh), notwithstanding the strong
opposition of the Burmese frontier authorities, secretly incited
by Mindon himself. Although he was forced by the Panthay
rebellion to return to Burma, his journey inspired the wildest
hopes. Fytche wrote to the Viceroy of India that Burma
promised 'to furnish a highway to China' and after alluding
to the threat of American competition, urged that Britain
'should be in a position to substitute a western ingress to
China.'

The enthusiasts went so far as to advocate the construction
of a railway line through Burma to Shanghai. The Government
of India, however, was strongly opposed to any attempts at
expansion in this direction. Lord Lawrence had viewed Sladen's
expedition with disfavour. His successor, Lord Mayo, replied
to Fytche's letter that the scheme, 'whatever its merits', was a

generation too early. Hopes were damped also by the disappointing results of the opening of steamer trade to Bhamo.

They revived in 1874, when Lord Salisbury became Secretary of State for India, and, in response to a petition from the British Associated Chambers of Commerce, ordered a fresh survey to be made. Hence was undertaken the double expedition of Colonel Horace Browne from Bhamo and Augustus Margary from Shanghai. Margary reached Bhamo in January 1875 before Browne's departure. He then started back ahead of the Bhamo party in order to make arrangements for them. But on 21 February, 1875, he was murdered by tribesmen at Manyine, halfway to Tengyueh, and the expedition was called off.

This was the last attempt made during the period of the Burmese kingship to penetrate China by the Bhamo route. The British agents, sent to Yunnan to investigate the Margary murder, reported that the route was unsuitable for railway construction. The difficulties also, which arose after Thibaw's accession in 1878, caused the withdrawal of the British Residents from both Mandalay and Bhamo, and for the time being attention was once more transferred to the Moulmein route.

Mindon Min is regarded by the Burmese as the best of his line. He made a start at modernizing the administration by substituting the European system of fixed salaries for the old custom of assigning districts for the maintenance of the higher officials. To raise the necessary revenue for this reform he introduced the *Thathameda* tax, by which houses in every district and town, except the capital, were assessed according to the situation, wealth and prosperity of the area. The average amount for the whole kingdom was worked out on the basis of ten rupees per household. The assessment might vary from year to year, and such factors as a failure of the monsoon rains or the destruction of a village by fire were taken into consideration. It was a notable advance on previous practice and appeared to be so well suited to the Burmese social system that it was retained by the British after the annexation of Upper Burma.

Mindon was also a fervent Buddhist. He had the text of the Law engraved on 739 marble slabs and placed round the Kuthodaw Pagoda at the capital. In 1871 he achieved the dearest wish of his life by convoking at Mandalay the Fifth

Buddhist Council in history. There in the presence of a vast concourse of monks the Bidagat Thonbon (Three Baskets of the Law) was solemnly recited. A decision was also taken to erect a new spire on the Shwe Dagon Pagoda at Rangoon. It was probably intended as a nationalist demonstration uniting all Burmese Buddhists in allegiance to the king. The British authorities permitted the ceremony on the understanding that the king himself should not be present, and a magnificent new *hti* ('umbrella') studded with jewels to the estimated value of £62,000 was erected by Mindon's envoys amidst the greatest rejoicings.

Mindon's relations with the British, notwithstanding his early disappointments, were always correct. He was by no means an anglophile, though his relations with some of the British administrators, with whom he came into contact, were particularly cordial. A few he treated as personal friends. But with great astuteness he strove to build up relations with foreign states, especially France and Italy, as a counterpoise to British power. The Kinwun Mingyi's mission to Europe is well known, not only because he was the first minister of the Hlutdaw ever to visit England, but also because of the diary he kept of his experiences. Although he was personally received by Queen Victoria, his visit did little to improve Anglo-Burmese relations, since on the way to London he negotiated treaties with Italy and France. And as Britain was becoming very uneasy about French designs in Indo-China, she became decidedly suspicious of French intrigues with the Court of Ava.

The French at once sent out the Comte de Rochechouart to obtain ratification of the document signed in Paris, but the negotiations broke down over the Burmese refusal to allow them to work the ruby mines of Mogok. The French on their part were wary of the Burmese desire for a full alliance providing for the import of arms. Fytche's treaty of 1867 had permitted Mindon to import arms with the sanction of the Chief Commissioner of British Burma, but his applications for rifles had been refused. He had therefore some excuse for seeking French aid. But in the existing state of Anglo-French relations he was playing with fire.

This incident illustrates the deterioration of Anglo-Burmese relations towards the end of Mindon's reign. There were three other causes of friction, the royal monopolies, the Karenni question and the 'Shoe question'. In Fytche's treaty the king had promised to abolish all monopolies save those on rubies, earth-oil and timber. In actual practice the royal control over purchases was applied to most of the important export products such as cotton, wheat, palm-sugar, pickled-tea, cutch and ivory, and was used in such a way that the exporter had to pay substantially above the open market rates for these commodities. The king's agents also bought rice in the Delta and piece-goods in Rangoon, and annoyed the merchants of that city by dealing directly with Calcutta if their prices were too high. It is not without significance that long before the deposition of Thibaw the Rangoon Chamber of Commerce was agitating for annexation.

On the east the British frontier running across Burma ended about halfway between the Sittang and the Salween at the western boundary of a hill tract known as Western Karenni, the home of the fierce and backward Red Karens. They claimed independence of the Court of Ava and Lord Dalhousie had recognized their claim. But their slave-raids, which, it will be recalled, were the cause of the establishment of the original Burmese stockade at Toungoo, led to constant friction between the British and Mandalay. In 1873 Mindon sent troops to occupy the tract, and, when the British objected, claimed suzerainty over the Red Karens. The matter was settled in 1875, when Sir Douglas Forsyth negotiated an agreement whereby the independence of the Karens was recognized by the Court of Ava. It was a bad arrangement, which did nothing towards stopping the raids from which British as well as Burmese territory suffered. It has been hinted that British solicitude for Karen independence was inspired by the fact that their land contained valuable teak forests. But when Dalhousie had originally laid it down that they were to be protected against future Burmese encroachment, this factor does not seem to have influenced him.

Forsyth's mission proved to be a turning-point in Anglo-Burmese relations. On his return from Mandalay he protested strongly against the indignity of having to take off his shoes and

sit upon the floor at royal audiences. In that same year the
Prince of Wales, later Edward VII, made his official tour of
India, and Burmese envoys went to Calcutta to greet him. At
their reception they were permitted to wear their shoes and sit
on chairs. Thereupon in an attempt to force Mindon's hand
instructions were issued that in future the British Resident was
to refuse to take off his shoes in the royal presence. As Mindon
dared not give way, no British Resident could again be received
in audience by a Burmese king. This loss of direct contact had
disastrous effects.

Mindon died in 1878 without designating a successor. After
the murder of the Kanoung Min in 1866 he had been afraid to
appoint another Heir Apparent, although repeatedly urged to
do so by the British Resident. The most popular candidate, the
Nyaungyan Prince, was eminently suitable. Just before the king's
death, however, he heard that a palace plot was afoot to place the
Thibaw Prince, a nonentity, on the throne, and, fearing for his
life, took sanctuary with his younger brother at the British
Residency. The Kinwun Mingyi sent an urgent request for
their surrender. Most unwisely the Resident refused, and the
two princes were deported to Calcutta. Thus the one chance of
securing the throne for the best candidate was lost.

The dying king's only suggestion was that three of his sons
should be nominated as joint rulers, but the Kinwun Mingyi
and his colleagues refused to consider so unprecedented a
measure, believing that civil war would be the inevitable result.
Instead, they fell in with the plot to make Thibaw king. They
planned to take power into their own hands and establish a
system of ministerial control; and even the British Resident in-
dulged in the fond hope that by this means a more constitutional
form of government would come into being. Should Thibaw
prove troublesome, they proposed to supplant him with their
own candidate.

Thibaw, however, was completely under the influence of his
domineering young wife, Supayalat, who saw through the
Kinwun Mingyi's manœuvre, and set herself to thwart it by
prevailing upon her husband to order the massacre of a large
number of the royal family on the plea that there was imminent
danger of an insurrection. In this atrocious deed the Kinwun

Mingyi and his party acquiesced in the mistaken belief that it would simplify their task of developing control over the king; and when the disillusioned Resident Shaw vigorously protested, he was told by the Kinwun Mingyi that a Burmese king was an independent sovereign, who had a right to take such measures as were necessary to prevent disturbances in his own country.

Disillusionment, however, was soon the lot of the ministerial party also, for Supayalat proceeded to place her minions, notably the ruthless Taingda Mingyi, in key positions in the palace, and to secure the dismissal of any minister whom she distrusted. And although Thibaw dared not dismiss the Kinwun Mingyi, through fear of revolt, the palace clique surrounding the queen became the dominating influence in the government.

The reaction of British Indian opinion to the massacre was so unfavourable that at first something like panic occurred at the Burmese Court. Lord Lytton, the Viceroy, reinforced the British garrison in Burma and urged the Home Government to take a strong line, even at the risk of war. But Britain was already at war with the Zulus and the Afghans, and trouble was brewing with the Boers of South Africa. The Government of India was therefore told that its attitude must be that of extreme 'forebearance'.

Nevertheless both Calcutta and Rangoon became most uneasy regarding the safety of the Residency. An armed steamboat was kept at the frontier ready to rush aid in case of trouble. In April and May a couple of anti-British incidents were taken so seriously that when Shaw died in June of that year no one was appointed to succeed him. Mr. St. Barbe, who took over as *Chargé d'affaires*, lived in a state of blockade and it was firmly believed that Thibaw cherished the design of massacring the inmates of the Residency. When therefore in September 1879 Sir Louis Cavagnari, the British Resident at Kabul, was murdered by the Afghans, St. Barbe and his whole staff were hurriedly withdrawn from Mandalay.

The Court of Ava, however, suddenly sobered by the realization that the closing of the Residency was an extremely drastic step, made a rather lame attempt to restore the situation by deputing an ambassador to Calcutta. He got no farther than the British frontier. There he was told that unless he were empowered to negotiate a new treaty with the Government of

India, it was useless for him to proceed. After waiting six months in vain at Thayetmyo, while the question of his powers was debated between Calcutta and Mandalay, he returned home.

A second opportunity to settle relations occurred in 1882. It arose over the Kabaw Valley question, which was thought to have been settled by Burney in 1834, when the valley had been awarded to Burma. Unfortunately no precise demarcation of the boundary line with Manipur had ever been carried out. With Thibaw's accession the Burmese fomented a series of frontier disturbances. The Government of India thereupon invited Thibaw to join in a frontier commission. When he refused, a British commission proceeded to mark out the frontier, and, in doing so, requested the Burmese to withdraw an armed guard from a village which was claimed by Manipur. In 1882 Thibaw sent an envoy to Calcutta. He was given a most favourable reception by Lord Ripon; but just when hopes of a friendly settlement were beginning to rise, Thibaw suddenly recalled him, and took up such a threatening attitude that in 1884 British reinforcements were sent to the Raja of Manipur. The frontier disturbances immediately ceased, but the hoped-for improvement in Anglo-Burmese relations faded out.

Meanwhile difficulties were multiplying in Upper Burma. Dacoity became rife, the Kachins of the north rebelled, Chinese guerrillas burnt Bhamo, and most of the feudatory Shan saw-bwas threw off their allegiance to Thibaw. There were serious attempts by members of the royal family to dethrone him. The Myingun Min and the Nyaungyan Min were both strong candidates, and one or the other might have succeeded, had they not been interned, the former by the French and the latter by the British. In 1884, when a movement in favour of the Myingun Min was suspected, further massacres occurred in the Mandalay Palace, which led to loud demands for annexation from the British and Chinese mercantile communities in Rangoon. Lytton was no longer Viceroy, the Government of India had changed its mind regarding intervention, and Sir Charles Bernard, the High Commissioner of British Burma, was strongly opposed to annexation. He believed that it would be deeply resented by Burmese opinion in British Burma, that it would have a disturbing effect upon the Indian Princes, and that it would entail a difficult and expensive 'pacification' afterwards. In his opinion the problem could best be solved by the succession of the Nyaungyan Prince, who was high-minded and intelligent. Unfortunately in the following year the prince died, and at almost the same time French policy towards Burma took a decided turn, which forced Britain to abandon the attitude of 'forbearance'.

Thibaw's *volte face* over the Manipur negotiations seems to have been the result of a decision to resume relations with France. He knew that Britain had become extremely uneasy about French activities on the Mekong and their penetration into Annam and Tongking. He imagined that he could play off the French against the British. It never occurred to him that in the dangerous world of power politics, in which he was living, his only chance of survival as an independent monarch lay in cultivating British friendship: that an approach to France might force the British to depose him.

In May 1883 he sent a mission to tour Europe, ostensibly for the purpose of collecting information regarding industry and science. Its real object was to seek an agreement with France for the import of arms. Jules Ferry, the French Foreign Minister and the guiding spirit in the French movement of expansion in Indo-China, was asked by the British Ambassador to guarantee that, in the event of a Franco-Burmese agreement being concluded, no facilities would be granted for the purchase of arms, and gave full assurances. In January 1885 Ferry informed the British Ambassador that a purely commercial treaty had been concluded with Burma, that it involved the appointment of a French consul at Mandalay, but contained no military or political clauses.

This announcement put the British very much on the alert. In May M. Frederic Haas arrived in Mandalay to take up his duties as consul, and it soon became obvious that very extensive concessions, clearly opposed to British interests, had been promised, and that even more were in the air. In July the Secretary of State for India told the Indian Government that under the terms of the agreement the French were to establish a bank at Mandalay and to finance the construction of a railway from Mandalay to Toungoo in British Burma.

Rumour also reported other schemes. The French were to take over the management of the royal monopolies, control the postal system, run river steamers in competition with the Irrawaddy Flotilla Company, open up overland trade with Tongking, and obtain the lease of the Mogok and Kyatpyin ruby mines. To cap it all, at the beginning of August news leaked out that Ferry had secretly given a written pledge to the Burmese envoys in Paris to the effect that, as soon as peace and order were established in Tongking, arms would be supplied to Burma through French Indo-China.

In face of all this even the Chief Commissioner changed his mind and expressed the opinion that unless the proposed concessions were abandoned, there would be no alternative to annexation. The danger of immediate French action, however, was already passing. Ferry was no longer in power: a revulsion of feeling against his ambitious policy had forced his resignation in the previous March. Moreover, France had suffered a series of reverses in Tongking, and was fighting a war with China and another in Madagascar. Hence, when Lord Salisbury confronted the French Ambassador in London with a copy of Ferry's secret promise of arms to Burma, and told him plainly that Britain could not agree to the proposed French concessions, the French Government repudiated all Haas's acts and in October removed him from his post.

It was one thing for the French to change their policy, but quite another for Thibaw, who, at the moment when France so suddenly climbed down, was fully committed to a course of action against a British commercial firm, which was the direct consequence of his agreement with France. He was left 'holding the baby' and the British were presented with the perfect opportunity for dealing firmly and finally with him.

The Bombay Burmah Trading Corporation with its head-quarters at Rangoon had for many years worked the Ningyan teak forests in Upper Burma under a contract with the Mandalay Government. Thibaw, in urgent need of money, and with a view to transferring the Corporation's contract to a French syndicate, accused it of extracting more than twice the number of logs paid for, of bribing the local officials, and of failing to pay its Burmese employees. The case went before the Hlutdaw, which fined the Corporation an amount equivalent in English money to £146,666 and ordered it to pay a further sum of £33,333 to the foresters. Harvey, with some justification, calls the case a 'false' one, since its object was not to secure justice. Furnivall, from a study of British documents, is inclined to think that there were some grounds for the charge.

The Hlutdaw's decision was published in August 1885, and was at once reported to the British Cabinet. On 28 August the British Government asked the Court of Ava to submit the matter to arbitration. No reply was vouchsafed by Thibaw's Government until the middle of October, when, still hoping for French support, it summarily rejected the British proposal. Thereupon on 30 October the Government of India despatched a steamer to Mandalay with an ultimatum due to expire on the evening of 10 November. The Court of Ava sent a blustering reply, refusing to reopen the case against the Corporation, but inviting the reappointment of a British Agent. This was taken as a rejection of the terms and the army was ordered to advance to Mandalay. Operations began on 14 November, and, after an almost bloodless campaign, Mandalay was occupied on 28 November and Thibaw surrendered.

It is possible to argue that Burma neither threatened nor was prepared for war, that the Burmese reply to the British ultimatum did not close the door to further negotiations, and that the British forced on the war because French difficulties in Tongking and elsewhere presented them with a heaven-sent opportunity to clinch matters with Burma. But these are really unimportant questions compared with the real issue. Furnivall sums the situation up succinctly when he says that the annexation must be regarded as an episode in the rivalry of Britain and France for supremacy in South-East Asia, "and can best be justified as removing at an opportune moment a potential cause of a European war".[1] The most significant statement in the Burmese reply to the British ultimatum was not its refusal to reopen the Bombay-Burmah Corporation case, but the challenging assertion that friendly relations with France, Italy and other states "have been, are being and will be maintained".

[1] Furnivall, J. S., *Colonial Policy and Practice*, p. 70.

CHAPTER XV

BURMESE ORGANIZATION UNDER THE KINGS

THE Burmese governmental system, as it existed under the Kongbaungset Dynasty, has been well described in its main features by European visitors. The central government is fully described in existing Burmese records such as the *Lawka Pynha* or *Inyon Saok*, which explains the appointment and duties of ministers and the etiquette of court ceremonies. No such records exist for the Pagan or Toungoo dynasties, but as everything was governed by the strictest possible regard for precedent, and there is reason to believe that the procedure under Alaungpaya and his successors was modelled on that of Bayinnaung, one may conclude that the Toungoo kings in their turn framed their court as closely as possible on the traditions of Pagan. The general lay-out of the palace indeed remained substantially the same from the eleventh century to the nineteenth.

The apex of the whole governmental pyramid, as in all other monarchies of Indo-China, was the king, whose theoretically unlimited claims to power were rigidly circumscribed by custom and etiquette. All royal letters begin with descriptions of him in much the same terms as the following: "The Burmese Sovereign of the Rising Sun, who rules over the country of Thunaparanta and the country of Tambadipa, with all the great dominions and countries and all the Umbrella-bearing Chiefs of the East, whose glory is exceeding great and excellent, the Master of the King Elephant, Saddan, the lord of many White Elephants, the Lord of Life, the eminently just Ruler." The words 'Thunaparanta' and 'Tambadipa' are corruptions of Sanskrit terms used by ancient Indian writers to describe parts of Further India reputed to produce gold and copper respectively. But whatever significance they had had in earlier times had been completely lost by the time of the Konbaungset dynasty, when, according to Burney, Thunaparanta meant all the countries to the northward of Ava and Tampadipa all to the southward.

All royal orders were issued through the supreme council of
the realm known from the building within the Palace enclosure,
in which its daily sessions were held, as the Hlutdaw ('place of
release'). It registered royal edicts, issued royal letters according
to the prescribed forms, and tried the most important cases.
In theory the king presided over its meetings, and his throne
stood in the council-chamber. In his absence either the Heir
Apparent or the senior Wungyi presided.

The Wungyis ('bearers of the great burden'), the highest
officials of the realm, composed the Hlutdaw. They were normally four in number, but in later days sometimes six. Referred
to by the title Mingyi ('great ruler'), each was a sort of Secretary
of State and had his own individual seal. Together they controlled
every department of government; but there was no distribution
of departments among them individually, as in the case of Siam.
Their decisions were recorded by a number of Sayedawgyis
('great royal writers') or by Thandawzins ('heralds') of the
household, whose function it was to deliver them to the
Atwinwuns ('Wuns of the Interior') for submission to the king.

The Atwinwuns are best described as privy councillors.
Their number varied from four in the eighteenth century to
eight towards the end of the monarchy. They occupied the
Byedaik ('bachelors' quarters') in the palace, once allotted to the
king's young men. Though of lower rank than the Wungyis,
they tended to exercise greater influence through their closer
proximity to the royal person. Two of them by rotation were
always in attendance upon the king night and day.

The Wungyis were assisted by a number of Wundauks
('props'), one of whom would be in attendance at the Hlutdaw
all night to receive royal orders. Every morning a Wungyi and
a Wundauk would meet the two Atwinwuns in attendance upon
the king to discuss any matter that was to be brought to his
notice, and would accompany them to the royal presence.
Wundauks were often employed on business of greater importance, or were sent as envoys on special missions.

Of intermediate rank between the Wundauks and the
Sayedawgyis were four Nakandaws ('royal listeners'), who
carried messages between the king and the Hlutdaw. Crawfurd
calls them 'authorized spies'.

The most important duty of the Thandawzins was to read aloud official letters and petitions at royal audiences. They also took royal messages to the Hlutdaw. When a Thandawzin arrived at the Hlutdaw with a royal message, all present turned towards the empty throne and shikoed while the Thandawzin, kneeling before it, read the contents of his documents in ceremonial sing-song. As officers of the Byedaik the Thandawzins became numerous and important in Mindon's reign, since his system of state monopolies was largely run through that body.

The Hlutdaw was the supreme court of appeal from the provincial courts and from the two courts at the capital, the Yondaw and the Tarayon. The former, presided over by the Myowuns, dealt with criminal cases. Cases of treason might be investigated there by a higher official such as a Wundauk or even a Wungyi. The Yondaw was also a sort of town hall. Royal orders affecting the city were published there. A Myowun was on duty there all night, and in case of fire or civil disturbance it was the rendezvous for officers of government.

The Tarayon, a smaller building close to the Yondaw, with two Tarathugyis in daily attendance, heard all civil suits, except such as were of too great importance by reason of the sum of money at stake, or because foreigners were involved. These were reserved for the Hlutdaw.

Cases arising within the Palace walls were normally dealt with by the Atwinwuns sitting in the Anauk-yon ('Western Court'). The Treasury (Shwedaik, 'gold building'), so important an organ of administration in Europe, was of considerably less importance than the Hlutdaw or the Byedaik, probably because most of the revenue was paid in kind. Unlike most in the Court of Ava the permanent officials on its staff were hereditary. It was also the record office where the state archives were housed.

Besides all these officials of ministerial and sub-ministerial rank there were various offices of distinction such as those of the Asewun (Paymaster-General), Pabewun (Master of the Ordnance), Thenat Wun (Infantry Commander), Amyouk Wun (Artillery Commander), Myin Wun (Cavalry Commander), and Hlethin Atwinwun (Commander of the war-boats), all of which were held by leading statesmen.

Throughout Burmese history until Mindon introduced the

payment of fixed salaries, officials of all classes were remunerated by a system similar to feudal sergeantry. The higher ones were granted the revenues of districts, the lower ones assignments of land on the royal domain. Royal princes and Wungyis were known by the districts, which, in common parlance, they 'ate'. Such is the origin of the names of the last four kings of Burma, Tharrawaddy Min, Pagan Min, Mindon Min and Thibaw Min.

The country was subdivided into provinces, townships, circles and villages, but by no means in the neat pyramidal order that the words suggest. Provinces often took their names from the *myo*, or fortified town, in which the Governor or Myowun resided. They were of very unequal size. The Myowun had entire responsibility for the civil, judicial, military and fiscal administration of his province. As the *myo* would usually be situated on a river, his deputy took the title of Yewun ('Water Wun'). Together with him two other high officials, the Akunwun ('Collector of Taxes') and the Akaukwun ('Collector of Customs'), formed the council of the Myowun, sitting at the Yondaw, or provincial headquarters, for public business of all kinds.

Judicial business was presided over by a sitkè, who acted as principal conservator of peace. Provincial officials were divided into two grades, the higher ones appointed by the crown, the more subordinate ones holding office by hereditary succession. The chief of these latter was the thugyi, who was the hereditary chieftain of a tract called in some places a *myo* in others a *taik*, conveniently rendered into English as 'circle'. It comprised a number of villages, each under a *gaung* (headman) appointed by the thugyi. The only clear picture of the system comes from Upper Burma. In Lower Burma war and rebellion had caused the complete breakdown of social order by the time of Bodawpaya's revenue inquests, which provides our main source of information. The Burmese chronicles record that the old kingdom of Pegu was divided by King Razadarit (1385–1423) into three provinces, each with thirty-two *myos*. But many of these were shown as jungle in Bodawpaya's revenue inquests, and there seems to have been no village life over much of Lower Burma.

The Myothugyi was the backbone of the social administration in Upper Burma. Society was divided into two classes, the ahmudan, liable to regular service, and the athi, liable to be recruited only in an emergency. The ahmudan were enrolled either in regiments or according to their particular form of non-military service, e.g. hereditary palace cooks. They normally lived in regimental villages cultivating the land allotted to them for their subsistence. The Myothugyi, as the regimental commander, exercised a sort of feudal lordship over the members of his regiment, collecting their revenue and settling their disputes. In criminal matters, on the other hand, his jurisdiction extended over all the inhabitants of his circle, whether belonging to his regiment or not. Our knowledge of the system is meagre. The records concerning it are defective, and come from the period when it was in decay. The facts which emerge clearly are that society was organized on a quasi-feudal basis, that the Myothugyi, a military commander by heredity, largely controlled the administration of his area, which included a number of villages. There was, however, no village system of the sort found in India.

The best contemporary account of the old Burmese fiscal system is Crawfurd's. By contrast with the liberal principles, which he and his former colleague, Raffles, had imbibed, it was "the most faulty and most mischievous part of the whole administration . . . replete with uncertainty, rapacity and violence". Being mainly customary it was even more chaotic than the picture of England presented by Domesday Book, since the burden of taxation was spread so widely that, as Furnivall writes, "almost every form of productive activity was taxed: the cultivation of rice land and gardens, sugar-boiling, fishing, the manufacture of torches and the collection of forest produce". The petroleum wells of the Yenangyaung district paid a five per cent duty on the oil extracted, the silver mines were rented by Chinese contractors, the ruby mines had to present the king with every stone worth more than 100 ticals.

There were no market tolls, but through the *pwezas*, who assayed all payments in silver, a purchase-tax was levied. In theory there were no excise duties, because the consumption of alcoholic liquors was illegal; but foreigners were exempted from the prohibition by the purchases of licences from local officials. Customs duties were payable on such imports and

exports as were permitted, while European vessels entering
Burmese ports were liable to a long list of additional charges,
most of which were the perquisites of local officials.

The actual amounts, which found their way into the Royal
Treasury, were very small by European standards. The total
amount there at the time of Bodawpaya's death in 1819 was
equal to £575,000. But in those days the king was called upon to
make few money payments; his officials, as we have seen, were
remunerated by assignments of lands and revenues or by fees
and commission. The extortion and embezzlement, of which
there were so many complaints, sprang almost entirely from the
pernicious system of perquisites, in which every official from the
highest to the lowest was involved. They preyed upon the
people, says Crawfurd, like a horde of locusts.

In the courts civil procedure was largely by precedent, and
although a Burmese version of the old Hindu code of Manu
was used, the influence of indigenous custom predominated.
The whole spirit of the procedure, not merely its form, was
strange to the earliest British administrator, who had to run
such a court. "He failed to understand," says Furnivall, "that
Burmans went to court to find a man of wisdom and authority
who could help them in arriving at an amicable settlement of
their disputes; that the various officials, who tried cases,
jointly or separately, in person or by deputy, in court or in their
private house, were (according to English notions) arbitrators,
and that the so-called codes were compilations by jurists, used
for guidance but not for literal application."[1] This idealized
version of what took place should be read along with Crawfurd's
view that "no prudent person enters into a lawsuit".

In criminal cases cruel punishments involving mutilation
and various horrible forms of death were not uncommon. In
such cases torture might be applied to both principals and
witnesses, while gaolers were known to use it in order to
extort money. European observers noted various forms of
ordeal in use. Prison conditions were appalling; owing to the
flimsy structure of the buildings, every prisoner had to be kept
in the stocks. Henry Gouger, a British merchant, who was
imprisoned at the capital along with the American missionary,

[1] Op. cit., p. 31.

Adoniram Judson, wrote an account of their experiences which gives a horrifying picture of the inside of a Burmese prison.[1]

The Buddhist Church was controlled by the king through a Thathanabaing ('possessor of discipline') and a council of ecclesiastics and laymen, all of whom he appointed. The administration was concerned with monastic discipline and the management of endowments to monasteries and shrines. Organization was loose and monasteries were largely autonomous. As every king had received part of his education as a boy in a monastery, it was customary for him on his accession to invest its abbot with the authority of Thathanabaing. The country was divided into districts at the head of each of which was a Gaing Ok, whose task it was to settle disputes and maintain discipline. No monk as such could be dealt with by the secular authority. Where one was accused of a serious crime, however, a local magistrate might hold an inquiry and submit a report to the king. The council would then unfrock the offender and hand him over to secular justice.

Every village had its pagoda and at least one resident monk, who held office by invitation of the villagers. The village monastery was also its school, where boys were taught not only the beliefs and moral precepts of their religion, but also to read and write. It was the universal custom for boys to don the yellow robe and enter a monastery at the age of puberty, and remain there for a year or two under instruction. There was thus a high degree of literacy throughout the country, and especially in Upper Burma, where monasteries were more numerous than in the south.

The influence of the monkhood was vast, and although they never sat in the courts, the law-books which guided judicial decisions, were almost all compiled by monks. Burmese life centred round the religious shrines and the monasteries; and during the many times of disorder, when the civil government broke down, it was the Buddhist organization, loose though it was, which held society together. It has been well said that "without studying their Buddhism, their priesthood, and their religious observances it is impossible to acquire any true insight into the Burmese character".

[1] Gouger, H., *A Personal Narrative of Two Years' Imprisonment in Burmah.*

CHAPTER XVI

THE PLANTING OF BRITISH ADMINISTRATION

IN 1826, when the British assumed the task of ruling Arakan and Tenasserim, conditions were unsettled, and remained so for some years. In Arakan it was not until a widespread revolt was put down in 1836 that the country began really to settle down. There was less trouble in Tenasserim, though insurgents seized Tavoy and Mergui in 1830. At first the two provinces were separately administered under the direct supervision of the Governor-General of India; but Arakan was soon transferred to the Government of Bengal and its Superintendent subordinated to the Commissioner of Chittagong. The Indian system of administration was introduced there by officials with almost exclusively Indian experience. Tenasserim remained under the Governor-General until 1834, when its judicial and revenue branches were placed under Bengal. Up to 1843, however, the officers in charge of its administration came from neighbouring Penang and had had no previous experience of India. For quite a considerable time also the question of its retrocession to Burma was in the air. Hence there was little interference from India, and Burmese methods and practices tended to prevail.

The first civil Commissioner, A. D. Maingy, was instructed to govern according to local laws and customs, but to introduce, wherever possible, the principles of liberalism. These had been demonstrated by a new generation of East India Company's servants, the most notable of whom were Sir Stamford Raffles, Sir Thomas Munro and Mountstuart Elphinstone, and were soon to find their finest expression in the work of Lord William Cavendish-Bentinck as Governor-General of India (1828–35). Economic freedom, equality before the law, and the general welfare of the governed were their guiding principles.

Maingy, however, soon discovered that where there was a clash between liberalism and Burmese custom, the latter tended

138

to prevail, notwithstanding his efforts to promote the former. Thus, in dealing with the judicial system, his introduction of the jury proved a failure, and after some ten years it dropped out of use. And although according to liberal ideas justice should be free, he found himself forced back on to the Burmese practice in civil suits of imposing a ten per cent duty payable by the loser.

The Burmese law books, the *Dhammathat*, a Pali version of the Laws of Manu, and the *Yazathat*, a collection of precedents and rules established by various kings, he found too complicated; so he drafted a new code, under which the Commissioner, a Deputy Commissioner or an Assistant Commissioner was to be the sole judge in every court, assisted by a native officer skilled in Burmese law. Such a court was foreign to Burmese practice, which was rather of the nature of arbitration than of judgement by fixed legal principles. In course of time, however, with the appointment of Burmese gaung-gyoks or sitkès as judges and magistrates, the older methods came to prevail. Nevertheless the introduction of the rule of law did contribute much to the welfare of the people. Official oppression and extortion became illegal, banditry was far more energetically suppressed than ever before, and security of life and property became a recognized feature of the new regime. The British Indian penal code too, which supplanted the old Burmese system with its use of ordeal, torture and revolting punishments, was far more humane.

Maingy completely overhauled the revenue system. In order to pay officials fixed salaries it was necessary to raise a cash revenue in place of taxes in kind. He abolished taxes, which appeared to him to be a burden on trade, and the compulsory labour services, paid at half the market rate, which were a marked feature of Burmese rule. His chief source of revenue was a general tax on the produce of land, supplemented by the farming-out of gaming-houses and of opium and liquor shops. Under Burmese rule the land tax had represented about six per cent of the produce. Maingy fixed it initially at ten per cent. But this yielded inadequate revenue for the payment of salaries, and it was gradually raised to twenty-five per cent of gross produce. Even then he was forced to revive the Burmese practice of paying collectors by commission instead of by fixed salaries.

One important innovation, which he introduced for administrative convenience, became the basis for the procedure subsequently built up for the assessment of revenue and retained until the end of British rule. It was that of settling the revenue over a period of years instead of attempting an annual assessment. But even at the highest rate the revenue still continued to be inadequate, and Burmese methods were gradually reintroduced, even 'compulsive labour', as Maingy dubbed it. When in 1834 the Government of Bengal took over the revenue administration, it had become very similar to what it had been under Burmese rule.

The Calcutta Board of Revenue condemned the methods employed, especially the taxes on salt, teak and other produce; but as the total annual revenue for the province was then only four lakhs of rupees, and was quite inadequate for governmental. needs, interference was useless, and things continued as before. It is interesting to note how strongly Maingy's efforts to reform both the judicial and the revenue systems were influenced by the work of Raffles in Java. And although taxation was higher than under Burmese rule, and could be more firmly enforced, the higher prices, which the peasant obtained for his produce with the abolition of restrictions on trade, enabled him to bear the heavier burden.

So far as was possible Burmese officials were re-employed by the British. Of the subordinate officials the thugyi, the hereditary chieftain of a small district, was by far the most important. Maingy retained the thugyis, but tried to convert them into government officials, appointable and transferable at will. Under a method, which he named 'gradationary control', he graded them in three classes according to the number of districts under their control, and paid them fixed salaries. Beneath them were village gaungs with police duties and kyedangyis for the collection of revenue. This system also reverted to something very similar to the old Burmese practice, since it was impossible to supervise the thugyis closely, and they tended to retain their districts for life. 'Gradationary control' therefore broke down, payment by commission took the place of salaries, and the thugyi became once more what he had been, a local chieftain with the gaungs and kyedangyis as his retainers.

While local administration was thus reverting towards the old Burmese system, the higher civil service became more and more centralized after the Indian model. The method of direct rule was introduced as in Bengal. The province was divided into three large sections each under a European Deputy or Assistant Commissioner, who combined the duties of judge, magistrate and revenue collector. At first there was little interference from above. But in 1834 standardization on Indian lines, with all its multiplicity of forms and returns began to creep in.

With the departure of Maingy's successor, Blundell, in 1843, the pace was quickened, since the four officers, who successively held the office of Commissioner during the next ten years, all came from India and knew nothing of either the people or the language. The link between the European and native branches of the administration was the head native entitled gaung-gyok or sitkè. At first employed in a mainly advisory capacity, he was promoted after 1843, largely through the policy of 'native agency' enunciated by Bentinck some years earlier, to the position of a judicial officer, and was thus instrumental in carrying local administration into still closer conformity with traditional Burmese practice.

When Pegu was annexed in 1852 Phayre framed its administration on the Tenasserim model. The province was divided into five districts under Deputy Commissioners. These in turn were sub-divided into townships under myo-oks. Each township comprised a number of circles under taikthugyis who supervised the work of gaungs and kyedangyis in the villages. Phayre and his successor Fytche had both spent most of their previous careers in Burma. When, however, the latter retired in 1871, the office of Chief Commissioner was held for the next quarter-century by a succession of men, all of whom had been trained in India and were expecting to return there on promotion. The administration, therefore, developed more and more along the approved Indian lines. And as circumstances forced the gradual reorganization of the government into departments, so uniformity of administration tended to eliminate the indirect rule of earlier days.

Thus when it was found that the village police could not cope with the disorder, which troubled the new province for some years after annexation, a special police force had to be recruited. In 1861 an Inspector-General was appointed, and under the new system organized by him the Deputy Commissioner, instead of being the head of the police, was given the assistance of a Superintendent of Police, who for much of his work was responsible to the Inspector-General. In the same way jails, civil hospitals, sanitation and vaccination came in 1864 under an Inspector-General. A Public Works Department also came into existence under a Chief Engineer, a Forest Department, and finally a Department of Public Instruction.

Nevertheless up to practically the end of the nineteenth century the circle with its taikthugyi remained the chief unit of local government, and although on account of the great diversity in the size of the circles in Pegu, a good deal of amalgamation or division had to be carried out for the sake of administrative convenience, indirect rule remained the general practice for many years, and the life of the ordinary villager went on much as it had under Burmese rule.

The abolition of the Ava kingship and the formal annexation of Upper Burma on 1 January, 1886, presented the British with far bigger problems than the earlier annexations had brought. The first question to be decided was whether the new territory should form a protected state like Afghanistan or be brought directly under British administration. Lord Dufferin, the Viceroy, favoured the former solution, but it was found to be impracticable. The Hlutdaw was discredited, there was no suitable candidate able to maintain himself without British military assistance, and the country was too disorganized. So after a meeting between Lord Dufferin and Sir Frederick Roberts, the Commander-in-Chief, at Mandalay in February 1886, direct administration was decided on. Sir Charles Bernard became Chief Commissioner for the whole of Burma, the Hlutdaw was abolished, and a consultative body of former ministers was set up with the Kinwun Mingyi at its head.

The most urgent problem was that of disorder. Notwithstanding the fact that when the question of military operations against Thibaw had originally been discussed, Major-General Knox Gore had estimated that while only 500 men would be required to take Mandalay, ten times that number, in addition to the already reinforced Burma garrison, would be needed for the task of 'pacification', many people, including the Viceroy himself, had optimistically believed that the Burmese would welcome the 'coming of the Great Queen'. The Burmese army, however, refused to obey the order to surrender and carried on widespread guerrilla warfare. Local thugyis, notably Bo Shwe and Nga Hlau, led the resistance of scattered bands all over the country, and no less than five royal princes, each claiming the throne, held out in different regions. There was even a serious rebellion in Lower Burma. It took five years of hard campaigning to quell the resistance. The situation became so grave during the later months of 1886 that Sir Frederick Roberts had to transfer his headquarters from India to Burma from November 1886 to February 1887, and an army of 32,000 troops and 8500 military police was fully engaged.

For civil administration Upper Burma was divided into fourteen districts each under a Deputy or Assistant Commissioner with a Police Assistant. So far as revenue and civil justice were concerned, the original intention was for these to work through indigenous local agencies according to local methods. As in Lower Burma local administration was based on the circle with its hereditary headman, the taikthugyi, or, as he was more often known in Upper Burma, myothugyi. But Bernard's successor, Sir Charles Crosthwaite, who came with firmly fixed ideas of Indian administration, brought with him a draft scheme for breaking up the circles into villages. He thought that the degree of power exercised by thugyis, and the absence of village communities with recognized heads, were defects which should be remedied.

The rebellious state of the country played into his hands, since the thugyis were the chief leaders of resistance in Upper Burma, and had failed to suppress it in Lower Burma. The upshot of it all was the conversion of the village into an administrative unit by the Upper Burma Village Regulation of 1887 and the Burma Village Act of 1889. These two measures

imposed statutory duties concerning the maintenance of order
and the collection of revenue upon the headman and villagers.

It was some time before the evil results of the new system
began to show themselves, since the circle headmen were only
gradually abolished. Furnivall, from his long experience of
administration in Burma, examines them with much acumen.[1]
He writes that in the first place the villages had duties without
any compensating rights imposed upon them. In the second
place in order to combine adequate emoluments for the headmen
with efficient administration, a comprehensive scheme of
amalgamation had to be carried through after 1909. The merging
of villages which ensued, and led to a reduction in the number
of headmen by over 2000, made the 'village' a mere artificial
administrative unit. In the third place with the disappearance of
the circle headman the habit of referring serious disputes
between adjacent villages to his arbitration "so as to arrive at a
compromise according to known custom" tended to die out,
and "the mechanical logic of the law courts" was substituted.
"The popular self-government of Burmese times was replaced
by a foreign legal system," he comments. Whether the semi-
feudal power of the myothugyi is rightly termed 'popular self-
government', and further, whether it would have been possible
to develop the circle system of Burmese times into an institution
capable of carrying out the new duties necessarily imposed by
twentieth-century conditions, are somewhat debatable questions,
it might seem. Burma unfortunately possessed no institution
similar to the Javanese *desa* upon which a healthy local administration could have been based.

In the previous chapter stress has been laid upon the
importance of the Buddhist Church in Burmese life. Burma
was *par excellence* a Buddhist state. From the earliest days of
annexation this situation was clearly recognized by the British
and, save under the stress of actual warfare, all possible respect
was shown to sacred places and religious observances. When,
in the early days of the occupation of Tenasserim, the monks
complained that a monastic building was being used as an
armoury, it was restored to them. No attempt was ever made
to undermine the religion of the people. British policy was that

[1] Op. cit., pp. 74–6.

of *laissez faire*, so long as religious practice did not clash with the maintenance of law and order.

This negative attitude, inevitable as it was under the circumstances, had unfortunate results. The monastic establishment cut off from its headquarters at the capital, suffered in both discipline and cohesion. After the annexation of Pegu in 1852 the deterioration became more strongly marked, since at first there was a considerable exodus to Upper Burma, and many monasteries were deserted. Later on, when large numbers of people returned, many monks remained behind in the Kingdom of Ava, and there was little attempt to restore the monasteries which had fallen out of use. The census of 1891 shows that whereas under Burmese rule every Lower Burma village had its monastery, there was then only one to every three or four villages.

Perhaps the chief cause of decay was the British refusal to give official recognition to the Buddhist ecclesiastical code on the grounds that this would constitute the kind of interference with religion, which the Queen's Declaration of 1858 at the close of the Indian Mutiny had forbidden. It meant in practice that the power of the Buddhist authorities to maintain discipline almost disappeared. In 1884, when Colonel (later Sir Edward) Sladen was consulted regarding the possible effects of the annexation of Thibaw's Kingdom, he said that he hoped the mistake made in Pegu would not be repeated in Upper Burma, and urged that government should support the lawful authority of the heads of the Buddhist Church.

After the deposition of Thibaw, however, his advice went unheeded, notwithstanding strong pressure from responsible Burmese leaders. The Thathanabaing himself headed a deputation to Sir Frederick Roberts asking for confirmation of the jurisdiction of the ecclesiastical commission, which had operated under the kings. Three matters were involved, endowments, the holding of examinations in the Pali scriptures, and discipline. There was no difficulty over the first two; but over the third, while the British authorities were willing to recognize the appointment of the Thathanabaing, they would not invest him with any legal powers.

Furnivall sums up the resulting situation thus: "For some

years ecclesiastical causes were left for decision by the Order, but judicial decisions gradually brought them within the jurisdiction of the civil courts. In ecclesiastical, as in lay affairs, British law supplanted Burmese custom, the last vestige of a monastic autonomy disappeared, and with them the only effective machinery for regulating admission to the Order and expelling disreputable members."[1]

The years that followed were to see the gradual disintegration of the Order, and the monks, who had at one time been the cultural leaders of the people, tended to become, though with many notable exceptions, an ignorant, disorderly class, preaching sedition and creating unrest.

[1] Op. cit., p. 200.

CHAPTER XVII

BUREAUCRACY, DYARCHY AND SEPARATION FROM INDIA

For a generation or more after the reorganization of the administration consequent upon the reunion of Burma under one authority, the country remained a sort of arcadian backwater. Civil officers serving there ruefully referred to it as the Cinderella of the Indian provinces. From about 1890 until Saya San's rebellion in 1930 there was such internal peace as no drevious period can show, a high degree of prosperity, and a substantial increase in population.

Until the end of the nineteenth century there was littel change in the machinery of the central government, which functioned very much like that of any other Indian province, Great changes, however, were taking place in the outside world. which were to have their effects on Burma. A new era of economic competition had begun between the leading European powers; the rapidly expanding industries of Europe needed more and more raw materials from the tropics, and in consequence Big Business was demanding the more efficient exploitation of colonies. The creation of an adequate administrative machinery for this purpose became one of the foremost aims of government, especially from the days of Lord Curzon. Government took on new functions, developed new departments and services, and *laissez-faire* was abandoned. Nor was the reorganization all in the interests of economic development: social justice and native welfare were actively promoted, partly as a means of justifying colonial rule, but also largely because a new generation of administrators arose, who were genuinely concerned about such matters.

The transformation began in Burma in 1897 with the promotion of the Chief Commissioner to the rank of Lieutenant-Governor, assisted by a Legislative Council of nine nominated members, including five non-officials. Then in rapid succession came the creation of separate departments for Jails and

Hospitals in 1899, a Commissioner of Land Revenue in 1900, a
Chief Conservator of Forests in 1905, a Director of Agriculture
and an Excise Commissioner in 1906. The year 1900 saw the
establishment of a Chief Court of Judicature, followed five
years later by the creation of a Judicial Service designed to
relieve local officers of all their civil and some of their criminal
cases. From 1900 also there was a closer control over Public
Instruction and a considerable extension of state education.
In 1904, in an endeavour to counteract the disastrous increase
in rural indebtedness in the rice-growing areas, a Co-operative
Credit Department was set up. In 1906 separate Agricultural,
Veterinary and Fishery Departments were instituted, while in
1908 a Sanitary Commissioner was appointed and a Public
Health Department began to function. To link up all these
departments a large new Secretariat came into existence in
Rangoon, and bureaucratic government became the order of
the day.

In India municipal government began in the larger cities
just before the Mutiny, district boards in rural areas from about
1865. During the seventies and eighties English Liberalism was
seeking to foster the political education of Indians by developing
local self-government. Hence it was at the instance of the
Government of India that municipal institutions were introduced into Burma. In 1874 nominated municipal committees
were established in a few towns. Eight years later the number
was increased and the elective principle introduced. At first the
signs were hopeful: the townspeople welcomed the opportunity
of having a voice in the management of their own affairs.
Apathy, however, soon set in. The general set of rules for
municipalities, framed by the Government Advocate in 1881,
was far too rigid and ignored popular feeling. Towns began to
fear that the new institutions would lead to an increase in
taxation. Moreover, the fact that the urban population was
composed of four distinct communities, Burmese, Indian,
Chinese and European, each with its own separate interests,
often conflicting, rendered common action difficult. Only in
Rangoon, with a large European element, a higher proportion
of educated Asiatics than elsewhere, and a senior government
officer as full-time chairman, was the system reasonably success-

ful. And even there, owing to the enormous influx of Indian coolies, housing and sanitary conditions left much to be desired. Elsewhere such efficiency as there was came mainly as the result of pressure from above. Self-government in a real sense never developed.

In the rural areas District Councils were first set up in 1884, also at the instance of the Government of India. As an experiment in self-government they failed rather badly. A tight hold had necessarily to be retained over them by the local officer responsible for carrying out the policy of government. As local officers were subject to frequent transfers, they rarely had any opportunity of getting to know their districts thoroughly. The general result was inefficiency and inability to check corruption among the subordinate officials. In the villages, on the other hand, particularly in those happy in possessing racial homogeniety, local self-government achieved some success. Some ran their own bazaars, while some small towns even ran their own electric lighting systems without official intervention. Wherever a community existed with traditions of common action, self-government succeeded.

The transformation of the provincial government, which began in 1897, was carried a stage further under the Minto-Morley reforms of 1909, when the Legislative Council of Burma was increased in size to a membership of thirty with a non-official majority. But it had little real power. Resolutions could be moved, votes taken and questions asked, but the principle of popular election was not introduced, and no resolution had binding force on the government.

When in 1917 the British Parliament accepted the principle of responsible self-government as the ultimate aim for India, it was obvious to all who knew Burma that her people lacked the political experience and education necessary for working a democratic constitution on the western model. Largely for this reason the Montagu-Chelmsford Report proposed to set aside the problem of her political evolution 'for future consideration'. The proposal evoked an immediate storm of protest in the country. Burmese national sentiment, long dormant, suddenly awoke and began to show itself as a force to be respected. The nationalist General Council of Burmese Associations carried on intense political agitation, organized boycotts and demanded home rule.

The strength of national feeling took everyone by surprise. In 1921 therefore the Secretary of State for India recommended to Parliament that the 'dyarchy' granted to India by the Government of India Act 1919 should be extended to Burma, and the Government of Burma Act 1921 was passed to bring Burma into line with the other provinces of India. To work out the details of the new constitution a Burma Reforms Committee, presided over by Sir Frederick Whyte, visited the country, and although the G.C.B.A. condemned dyarchy as inadequate, Burma became a Governor's Province in 1923 and the new form of government was established, though the Shan States, Karenni and the Tribal Hills were excluded from its operation.

The Legislative Council was increased to 103 members of whom 79 were to be elected on a democratic franchise, 2 were *ex officio* and 22 nominated. The government was entrusted to a Governor with an Executive Council of two members in Charge of Reserved Subjects, and two Ministers, responsible to the legislature, in charge of Transferred Subjects. The reserved subjects comprised defence, law and order, finance and revenue. The transferred departments included education, public health, forests and excise. The transference of the Forest Department placed Burma ahead of all the other provinces of India except Bombay. The franchise was granted to householders without sex disqualifications and with eighteen as the minimum age limit.

Such were the outlines of dyarchy. Its most surprising feature was the franchise qualification, which fixed an age limit well below the practice of any European democracy. The reason for this is difficult to assess. "The official explanation was that no qualifications of age, property or education could be devised; simplicity welcomed it as evidence of faith in liberal ideals; cynics ascribed it to petulance, 'making the best of a bad job' or to astuteness—if the people do not like bureaucracy, let them have democracy in full measure to disillusion them. The kindest explanation is that the Government trusted, as it believed, the well-merited affection of the 'conservative element' against the disaffection of a few pernicious agitators." So writes Furnivall, who saw the inauguration of the new system.[1]

In the new legislature right from the start the opposition normally commanded greater voting power than the government, and was solidly nationalist. The procedure of the House was as closely as possible modelled on that of the British House of Commons, and the Burmese members learnt the new procedure with truly remarkable speed. The dominant party was the People's Party led by U Ba Pe, and often referred to as the 'Twenty-one Party' from the number of those who signed its first programme. There was also a smaller Independent Party, led by Sir J. A. Maung Gyi, which supported the government. A third party of extreme nationalists under U Chit Hlaing boycotted the Council.

There was no difficulty in obtaining candidates for ministerial posts, even from the opposition, and some curious situations resulted. But Ba Pe and his followers were moderates, anxious to use the Council for forcing on the government by constitutional means the reforms they had at heart. Their demands included better education to fit Burmans for self-government, rapid Burmanization of the public services, the promotion of indigenous economic development, the curtailment of foreign exploitation, the provision of more money for the 'nation-building' departments and for agricultural credit.

But the electorate was at first apathetic, and there were too many personal rivalries among the leaders for them to combine effectively to control the government. Hence, notwithstanding some notable progress, particularly in the spheres of education and public health, Furnivall's strictures cannot be gainsaid: "The condition of the cultivators deteriorated, racial tension became more acute, crime increased and disaffection spread." It is not fair, however, to saddle the new system with these failures. The newly elected legislators needed time in which to learn their job, and especially how to control an administrative machine without jamming it.

Finance was the crux of the situation and it was a reserved subject: if the nation-building departments needed more

[1] Op. cit., p. 160.

money, their heads had no responsibility for the additional
burden this would impose on the tax-payer. It was thus impossible to work out a nicely adjusted long-term policy, involving the co-operation of the government and the electorate,
and the big problems tended to be shelved on the plea of financial
stringency. It was not that the Finance Department's control
was unfairly used, but rather that in the dyarchical form of
government the co-ordination at the top, necessary for the
direction of a national policy was supremely difficult.

Yet dyarchy was by no means a façade; there were men of
goodwill on both sides who aimed at making it a real step
forward in the political education of the people. The ultimate
objective was dominion self-government. The step taken
towards it in 1923 was decisive: there could be no going back.

When in 1928 the 'Simon Commission' came to review the
working of the reforms instituted five years earlier, the almost
unanimous Burmese demand was for immediate full responsible
government and separation from India. The explanation of this
was simple. Burmese kings had deeply resented having to deal
with a viceroy; they wanted direct relations with the English
sovereign. Now Burmese nationalism made the same demand.
Faced by increasing Indian immigration and economic competition, the Burman feared that his country might one day
become a vassal state of an Indian commonwealth ruled by
Indians.

The Simon Commission reported in favour of separation;
but when, soon after the publication of its report, the Round
Table Conference met in London to discuss the framework of a
new Indian constitution to replace the dyarchy, the Burmese
delegates at the first session of the Conference were less forth-
right on the subject of separation. Before committing their
country they wanted assurances that her rate of constitutional
progress and her economic relations with India would not be
prejudiced. Burmese suspicions had been aroused by the
unqualified support given to separation by the European civil
services and business men.

The Anti-Separationists had made some headway by
suggesting that the best safeguard would be for Burma to join
the proposed Indian federation on the understanding that she

might secede if she so desired. The result was that when the special Burma Round Table Conference, held in London between November 1931 and January 1932, agreed on the main lines of a constitution for a Burma separated from India, an Anti-Separation League was formed which won a complete victory at the general election held in November 1932. In spite of explicit official assurances to the contrary, it was widely believed that the British advocated separation in order to keep Burma as a crown colony. At the same time hardly a single anti-separationist was in favour of permanent union with India. When therefore it was made clear that federation on a strictly temporary basis with the privilege of secession at will could not be entertained, opinion swung back in favour of separation, and the Government of India Act 1935 gave it legal force.

The constitution of separated Burma was outlined in Part XIV and Schedules X–XV of the act, and re-enacted in the Government of Burma Act 1935. It came into effect from 1 April, 1937. The Burma Government came directly under the British Parliament, the Secretary of State for India became Secretary of State for India and Burma, and a separate Burma Office was created under an Under-Secretary for Burma. At the head of the new government was a Governor solely responsible for defence, external and internal, monetary policy, currency and coinage, foreign affairs and the Excluded Areas of the Shan States, Karenni and the Tribal Hills. In all other matters, save certain emergency powers entrusted to his special responsibility, he was bound to act on the advice of his ministers. The general administration was directed by a cabinet of ministers, responsible to the legislature and under the leadership of a Prime Minister. Their number was restricted to ten; in practice it varied between six and nine.

The legislature consisted of a Senate, half elected by the House of Representatives and half nominated by the Governor and a House of Representatives. The House of Representatives contained 132 members of whom ninety-two were elected by territorial constituencies and the remainder represented communal and other special interests. The franchise was extended to about one-third of the male population and one-tenth of the female.

Even allowing for the Governor's 'reserved' powers and his 'special responsibility' powers, the Burmese Cabinet had effectual control over practically all internal affairs. It was in fact laid down that the 'reserve powers' were to be progressively restricted in the course of time, and it was understood that the Governor's 'special responsibility powers', which included the prevention of grave menace to internal peace, the protection of minorities and the prevention of unfair discrimination against British subjects or their goods, would as far as possible be held in abeyance.

The first general election was keenly contested, and in some constituencies two-thirds of the roll actually voted. Dr. Ba Maw, the first premier, and his cabinet showed themselves anxious to tackle such serious problems as agrarian distress, corruption and village administration. The difficulties ahead were vast, and it would have been interesting to have seen how the Burmese would have shaped up to them, now that they had what amounted to almost complete responsible government. But the peace of the world was already threatened by Nazi Germany, and Japanese penetration into China was assuming alarming proportions. Hence the conditions of external peace, so necessary for a new system to be given its chance to take root and grow, never really existed, and the period of barely five years, which elapsed between its inception and the Japanese conquest, must be judged with the greatest reserve.

CHAPTER XVIII

ECONOMIC AND SOCIAL EVOLUTION

WHEN Tenasserim and Arakan were annexed in 1826, their economic value was slight. Tenasserim had a very scanty population living mainly by subsistence agriculture, and the hope that the more settled conditions would induce the Mons to return from their refuge in Siam was soon disappointed. The province, however, possessed valuable teak forests, and by throwing them open to licensed private enterprise, the development of Moulmein into a thriving port with sawmills and shipbuilding yards was stimulated. Between 1830 and 1852 more than 100 ships with a total gross tonnage of over 30,000 tons were constructed there. But indiscriminate felling without proper supervision ruined many of the forests, and the rapid development of Rangoon after 1852 caused Moulmein's star to wane. Rangoon with the great waterway of the Irrawaddy behind it came almost to monopolize the sea-borne trade of Burma. Because of navigational difficulties on the Salween, Moulmein had little hinterland, and although strenuous efforts were made to open up overland routes with the Laos States and Western China, these were all found to be commercially impracticable.

Arakan had driven a considerable export trade in rice in the seventeenth century. Under Burmese rule much of its population had emigrated, and the export of rice was contrary to the policy of the Court of Ava. The removal of restrictions on import under British rule, and the proximity of the Indian market, caused the rice trade to revive. The alluvial plains of the Kaladan and Lemyo rivers produced the best rice in Burma, and Akyab soon became a commercial centre, which attracted British merchants.

Tenasserim had failed to pay its way, but Lord Dalhousie confidently expected that the acquisition of Pegu would more than redress the balance. In his plans Rangoon's future was envisaged not only as a great port but also as "one of the most beautiful cities and stations within the whole bounds of

India".[1] The Delta area was potentially rich, but largely uncultivated. Owing to the Burmese treatment of the Mons much of Lower Burma was depopulated and its social life decaying. The Second Burmese War caused a movement of population into Upper Burma, which continued for a short time after the return of peace. Hence in the early years of the annexation there were few signs of economic progress.

The Indian Mutiny of 1857–58 caused the first upward tendency in the rice production of the Delta. India's demand for rice stimulated an influx of population back from Upper Burma. Little by little cultivation was expanded, and rice supplanted teak as the staple export. It was easy to sell the surplus, the price was high, British rule put an end to extortion and oppression, and the old restrictions on freedom were removed. When the American Civil War cut off the Carolina rice supply, Britain looked to Burma to make up the deficiency, and rice cultivation for the external market began in earnest. The opening of the Suez Canal in 1869 was a further stimulus to production.

The colonization of the Delta, and the expansion of its rice production during the next seventy years, constitute the most spectacular development of Burma's economic history. The total acreage under paddy in the province rose from below two millions to nearly thirteen, and the rice export from below 400,000 tons to three and a half millions. The wild scramble for land, and the crying need for capital, led to a situation, which by the end of the third decade of the twentieth century had become acutely dangerous owing to the phenomenal growth of agricultural indebtedness. Indian moneylenders of the *chettyar* caste supplied most of the capital, and by 1930 the total agricultural indebtedness of Burma was estimated at the huge sum of £40 million.

Not only did peasant proprietorship break down, but during the years of rapid expansion the demand for labour was so great that numbers of Indian immigrants arrived, with a much lower standard of living than the Burmese. The result was that Indians undercut Burmans in competition for land tenancy. At the same time the multiplication of great steam-driven rice mills

[1] Hall, D. G. E., *The Dalhousie-Phayre Correspondence*, 1852–56, p. 394.

employing Indian coolies drove the small Burmese rice-millers out of the trade. Cheap Indian labour also drove the Burmese from the wharves, while the substitution of steam navigation for native craft, particularly on the rivers, forced many Burmese out of their traditional occupations.

Thus while in the earlier stages of the development of the Delta, when there was unoccupied land in abundance, the Burman prospered and his standard of living improved, in the later years through excess of borrowing, increase of competition for landholdings and the decline of domestic industries, he found his economic difficulties multiplying and his efforts to transfer to industry thwarted by Indian competition. It was only when the great world depression of 1929 onwards brought the price of rice tumbling down, and the startling fact was discovered that half of the occupied land of Lower Burma was in the hands of non-resident non-agriculturists, that the true magnitude of the problem revealed itself.

Government had realized soon after 1880 that all was not well with the peasant cultivator. In 1882 and 1883 attempts were made to save him from the clutches of the moneylenders by the passing of two acts to provide cultivators with loans at low rates of interest. But the conditions imposed were too stringent for the improvident Burman, who found the Chettyars easier to deal with, notwithstanding rates of interest rarely lower than twenty-five per cent.

Early in the twentieth century another attempt to check the evil was made by the encouragement of co-operative societies financed by land-banks. At first thousands of these societies were formed, but most of them failed, and with the depression of 1929 the two most important land-banks, the Burma Provincial Co-operative Bank of Mandalay and Dawson's Bank of Pyapon, ran into serious difficulties. By this time it was realized that a big effort at reconstruction was called for. Many co-operative credit societies were revived and by 1940 their number was rapidly increasing. From the end of 1935 it became possible with government sanction for foreclosed land to be returned to its original owners on payment of its market value spread over fifteen years. In 1936 a Debt Conciliation Act came into force, which established boards for scaling down debts and accumulated interest, while in 1937 one of the first acts of the new legislature was to pass a Burma Tenancy Bill, against strong Chettyar opposition, for the protection of tenants. Thus the period immediately preceding the Japanese conquest saw a real, if somewhat belated, attempt to grapple with what had become the most urgent internal problem.

Long before these measures were taken, however, dangerous communal discord had arisen. The first big outbreak was in 1930, and was directed against Indian coolie labour in Rangoon. At the beginning of the century Indians were arriving in Burma at the rate of 250,000 a year, and the number was rising steeply each year. In 1927 it touched the peak figure of 480,000. The majority did not settle in the country, but returned home in a year or two. Enough remained, however, for the proportion of Indians to the total population to show a clear increase in each decennial census. They not only swamped the labour market, but they almost monopolized such professions as the law, medicine, accountancy and engineering, and in the big business houses Indian clerks were preferred to Burmese. The riots of 1930 arose out of the use of Burmese labour to break a dockyard strike. When the Indians submitted, the Burmese objected to being dismissed and in three days of fighting killed 120 Indians and wounded 900.

At the end of the same year a formidable rebellion under a leader called Saya San broke out in Tharrawaddy district and spread rapidly over most of the Delta. Not until March 1932 was it finally stamped out. It was an anti-foreign movement, due largely to economic discontent arising out of the great slump. The majority of the rebels rose to recover their lands from the hands of the moneylenders.

This was not the only symptom of social disintegration; the same period was one of growing clerical disorder. In the last two decades of British rule many of the more unruly monks had become political agitators. They stirred up nationalist self-assertion in its worst forms, and introduced an element of intolerance into Burmese Buddhism which it had never previously known. The most striking manifestation of this spirit came in July 1938, when it was asserted, quite without foundation, that the Buddhist religion had been insulted by a

book published by a Mohammedan some years earlier. In many
districts throughout the country Burmese rioters attacked Indian
Muslims, killing and wounding hundreds. Monks played an
important part in these murderous outbreaks.

The economic and social problems, which beset Lower
Burma, were much less in evidence in Upper Burma. While the
Lower Burma agriculturist was almost exclusively concerned
with the production of rice, and was to an ever greater extent
after 1870 at the mercy of foreign markets and the monsoon, the
Upper Burma peasant produced a wide variety of crops, mainly
for subsistence. Small independent holdings were the order of
the day and cottage industries flourished. Surplus crops such
as vegetable oils and sugar cane found a ready market in the
south, and their sale enabled the Upper Burma peasant to
purchase important textiles and other consumer goods. Cotton
and beans also were grown partially for export. The great
variety of crops and the survival of small industries meant that
the peasant was less affected by vagaries of rainfall than the
Lower Burma rice farmer, who might be ruined by one bad
season.

The rubies of Mogok district had been famous for centuries,
but all attempts by Europeans to develop a satisfactory export
trade in the days of the kings had failed. Royal policy was
blamed for this. In 1889 a European Company took up the
lease of the mines at an annual rent of Rs315,000, but never
made much profit, and went into voluntary liquidation in 1931.

Much greater success attended the European exploitation of
the petroleum wells of the Yenangyaung region, which had for
many generations been worked by hereditary Burmese owners.
The Burma Oil Company, formed after the annexation of 1886,
at first purchased its oil from the native drillers, and confined
itself to the task of refining and distribution. Early in the present
century it began to apply modern methods of drilling and
large-scale production. In time it controlled three-quarters of
the industry and maintained a labour force of 23,000. Indians
at first formed the majority of this, but by 1937 Burmese
numbered sixty-one per cent of the total, and Burmese graduates from Rangoon University where the B.O.C. had founded an
engineering college were being regularly recruited for its

professional posts. In 1908 a pipe-line had been laid between the oil-fields and Syriam, where the main refineries were stationed. In the years just before the Japanese invasion the annual export of the Company's products was valued at £10 million, and its contribution to provincial revenues was £1¾ million. In terms of world production its output was only about .5 per cent of the total, but Burma was well placed for supplying the needs of eastern and southern India.

The twentieth century saw the development of other mineral resources, which gave Burma a far from inconspicuous place in world economy before World War II. The great Bawdwin mine, near Namtu and forty miles north-east of Lashio, once worked by the Chinese, became under the Burma Corporation the most important lead mine in the world and one of the chief sources of silver. There were few Burmese, however, in its labour force. Two other mining areas, at Mawchi in Karenni and in the Tavoy district of Tenasserim, placed Burma second only to China in the production of tungsten and fifth among world producers of tin. Here again Burmese labour played an infinitesimal part.

Thus while the first steps towards self-government were being taken by the Burmese, they were faced by the extremely disquieting fact that their country was being developed by foreign capital, brains and technicians, while at the same time in certain basic industries they were undercut by foreign labour. In only one sphere did they hold their own; they proved themselves excellent motor mechanics and drivers. In general, however, they were agriculturists and handicraftsmen, and their most bitter pill was that in the rich rice country of the south they themselves had become largely landless labourers. It is hardly to be wondered at that the third and fourth decades of the twentieth century witnessed not only the spread of social and political unrest, but also a crime wave of unprecedented magnitude.

Many Burmans looked to the spread of education as one of the most important roads to salvation. As in Siam also, monastic schools had for centuries given Burma a much higher rate of literacy than existed over most of the Far East; but their instruction went little further than reading, writing and simple arithmetic. It was upon the monastic schools that the British made their first attempts to build an educational structure. Phayre distributed text-books in arithmetic, geography and land-surveying to them, and sent round trained teachers to show the monks how to use them.

In 1866 the first Director of Public Instruction was appointed to supervise the scheme. Unfortunately he died soon after appointment, and his successor knew no Burmese. The original plan, therefore, met with little success. Then it was decided to substitute lay schools for monastic ones. Eventually both systems were worked simultaneously, and it is interesting to note that the number of recognized monastic schools increased much faster than that of the lay schools. Both types were encouraged by the payment of grants-in-aid or by rewards based upon examinations conducted by inspectors.

With the increase of government and European business a demand arose for clerks with a knowledge of English. The monastic schools were considered unsuitable for the teaching of English, and attention was directed to the establishment of Anglo-Vernacular schools. In this way in the seventies Government Middle Schools came into existence, while grants were made to mission schools run by the Roman Catholics, the American Baptist Mission and the Society for the Propagation of the Gospel. Some of these became sufficiently advanced to be affiliated to Calcutta University, and some of their best pupils took its matriculation examination.

In 1880 the system was overhauled, a Departmental Board of Examiners was set up to carry out annual provincial examinations, and nine standards of instruction, culminating in the Calcutta matriculation, were organized. One of the Anglo-Vernacular schools, Rangoon Government High School, founded in 1873, developed a higher department, which in 1884 became Rangoon College, and began to prepare students for the external degrees of Calcutta University. But very few government schools were founded. The policy laid down in the Education Code of 1891 was to assist, regulate and inspect voluntary schools, rather than found and maintain government ones.

By 1900 Government maintained five normal schools for

the training of teachers, two survey schools under the Department of Land Records and Agriculture, an elementary engineering school, founded at Rangoon in 1895, a vernacular forest
school at Tharrawaddy, Government High School, Rangoon,
Rangoon College, with arts and law courses only, and a school for
the training of midwives at the Dufferin Hospital, Rangoon. In
addition there were sixteen secondary schools run by various
missions, and a small American Baptist College in Rangoon,
mainly for the higher education of Karens, among whom
American missionaries had worked for over half a century with
conspicuous success. Throughout the country there were over
17,000 schools, most of them giving only primary instruction in
the vernacular. One hopeful feature was that 341 of them were
girls' schools.

In the twentieth century, notwithstanding Lord Curzon's
dictum that more attention should be paid to primary than to
secondary instruction, so great was the demand for clerks that
secondary schools were multiplied and monastic schools
declined. This naturally led up to the foundation of Rangoon
University in 1920. Before that date, however, some progress
had been made with professional and vocational education. In
1907 a medical school was opened in Rangoon for the training
of medical subordinates. There came also into being a Government Technical Institute at Insein, the Saunders Weaving
Institute at Amarapoora and the Government Lacquer School
at Pagan. But until the University was able to open departments
of medicine, engineering and forestry, higher qualifications in
these three callings had to be sought abroad, and the number of
Burmans able to afford the expense was very small. Worse still,
not until 1924, when the Mandalay Agricultural College was
opened, was there any real attempt to develop instruction on
western lines in Burma's most important industry.

In 1920, when the University came into being with its two
constituent colleges, University College (previously Rangoon
College) and Judson College (previously the American Baptist
College), the rapidly awakening political consciousness of the
Burmese had become alive as never before to the need for
educational progress. A demand for 'national education' found
expression in a widespread school strike, and an attempt, under

a Council of National Education, to create a complete educational system independent of government control. Existing establishments were accused of inculcating the 'slave mentality'.

The boycott movement, however, gradually lost vitality
when dyarchy was introduced. In 1923 one of its promoters
became the first Minister of Education. The University of
Rangoon, throwing off the shackles of Calcutta, began to rise
rapidly in the public estimation. Hence, when in 1924 a
University Amendment Act was passed, giving Burmans
greater control over it, the boycott was officially called off, and
the more efficient C.N.E. schools qualified for government
grants.

University education went ahead with great zest, particularly with the completion of the splendid modern colleges,
halls of residence, staff houses and other amenities on the
beautiful 450-acre estate at Kokine. With an able and enthusi-
astic staff, at first largely European, it built up high standards
in a human and friendly atmosphere. Its graduates notably
improved the standards of the services to which they secured
entry. But it soon began to encounter inevitable difficulties. Far
too few students passed through its scientific departments, far
too many drifted into law, while still more failed to stay the
course and left without degrees to become political agitators.
Very few indeed went in for research.

The Students' Union became a hotbed of political discontent, and to many students politics became more important
than academic studies. Over 700 went on strike in February
1936 as a protest against disciplinary action against two of their
number. Politicians never ceased to agitate for external degrees
on the Calcutta model, and although the average all-in cost of
university education was only about £50 a year, and some fifty
per cent of the students received scholarships or bursaries,
there were loud complaints that it was too expensive. Hence as
soon as the new constitution came into force in 1937, fresh
attempts were made to subject the university to political
control. In 1939 its constitution was revised and, when the
Japanese invasion came, it had already begun to show signs of
deterioration.

The old civilization of Burma developed along the banks of

rivers. The Burmese are still a riverine people, and in the
Delta nearly every family has its own boat. Before the advent of
steam navigation European visitors were fascinated by the
multitude and variety of the craft to be seen on the Irrawaddy.
Even in the most prosperous days of the Irrawaddy Flotilla
Company's monopoly of inland steam navigation it never
carried more than fifty per cent of the total river traffic. The
Company started in 1865. Under the treaty of 1867 with
Mindon Min it began to operate a weekly service to Mandalay
and a monthly one to Bhamo. Later on its boats plied on the
Chindwin as far as Homalin, close to Assam, and connected
Rangoon through the Twante Canal with all the more important
towns of the Delta. Some of its steamers were the largest
shallow-draft river craft in the world.

With water transport catering so fully for the needs of the
province, the need for roads hardly existed until the coming of
the motor-car. By 1918 there were only about 2000 miles of
metalled roads, though there were several thousand more miles
of bullock-cart tracks, mainly in areas less affected by the wet
monsoon.

The first railway, the Irrawaddy Valley State Railway, from
Rangoon to Prome, was opened in 1877, and did much to
increase rice production in the Hanthawaddy, Tharrawaddy
and Prome districts. It was followed in 1884 by the Sittang
Valley State Railway, which linked Rangoon with Toungoo.
Five years later it was extended to Mandalay, and in 1899 to
Myitkyina 722 miles north of Rangoon. In 1896 all the lines
were taken over by the Burma Railways Company under contract with the Secretary of State for India.

The Company opened in rapid succession a number of new
lines, the Northern Shan States line to Lashio, one from Thazi
to Myingyan, another from Sagaing to Alon on the Chindwin,
a branch of the Prome line to Bassein, and the Southern Shan
States line from Thazi to Heho. Later there were extensions
from Henzada to Kyangin, from Heho towards Taunggyi and
from Pegu to Martaban and Ye. Altogether in 1941 there were
2060 miles of railroad, all of metre-gauge. In 1929 the Company's agreement was terminated and the railways were taken
over by the state.

It seems at first sight strange that before the Japanese war there was no link up of the Burma railways with those of India, Siam or French Indo-China. Overland trade between India and China was practically non-existent, and Burma possessed no important overland communications with her neighbours. The natural outlet for the trade of Western China was eastwards down the great rivers to the Pacific, while, so far as Siam and French Indo-China were concerned, as their exports were almost exactly the same as those of Burma, there existed no economic demand for intercommunication.

After the Margary murder in 1875 the chaos of Thibaw's reign interrupted for some years British attempts to establish communications with Yunnan and Szechuan through Bhamo. Up to 1904 Anglo-French rivalry for the control of the Upper Mekong was intense. It was believed to be the key to the trade of Yunnan, the economic and strategic importance of which was still much exaggerated. During Thibaw's reign the old projects of using Moulmein as the base for overland communication with Western China was revived by Archibald R. Colquhoun and Holt S. Hallett, who after much prospecting advocated a plan for a railway across the Siamese frontier to Raheng, and thence to Szumao and Yunnan. But neither the king of Siam, who was suspicious of its political implications, nor the Government of India, distrustful of its economic soundness, would look at it; and in any case the annexation of Upper Burma in 1886 rendered it valueless.

This event, followed by the annexation of the Shan States previously under Burmese suzerainty, opened a new phase of Anglo-French competition on the Mekong. The demarcation of the frontier between Burma and French Indo-China caused much heart-burning on both sides, and in 1895 a serious quarrel over an incident in the little trans-Mekong state of Mong Hsing, not unlike the Fashoda affair slightly later. On this occasion Britain climbed down and handed over the state to France. In 1897 an Anglo-French agreement permitted the construction of a French Yunnan railway to be connected up with the Burma Railways; but nothing came of it. Between 1894 and 1900 Major H. R. Davies made a series of valuable surveys of possible railway routes to Yunnan. He reported that the

country was 'exceedingly difficult' and that the profits of such
a venture were doubtful. Lord Curzon went further and dubbed
the scheme 'midsummer madness'. Soon afterwards the
Entente Cordiale of 1904 brought the rivalry of the two nations
to an end, and for many years the question of an overland route
to China receded into the background.

In 1937 the situation suddenly changed. Japan attacked
Shanghai and began to blockade China's southern ports. The
Chinese Government at once set about building a lifeline to
link up with Lashio and Bhamo. A highway for motor traffic
was completed before the end of 1938, and became known to the
world as the 'Burma Road'. Work was also pushed on with the
construction of a railway, and in April 1941 it was announced
that the Northern Shan States line was to be extended from
Lashio to the Chinese frontier. Aerial communications also were
developed by the Chinese National Aviation Corporation,
which began to link up Chungking, Kunming and Rangoon by a
regular air service.

The Burma Road was an emergency war measure; its
economic value was slight. The addition of a railway might have
improved things considerably, but the Japanese conquest rendered the project stillborn. Burmese nationalist opinion, however, objected strongly to the road; it feared that the easy
entry which it would provide for Chinese immigrants might
also become a threat to Burma's independence.

CHAPTER XIX

THE JAPANESE CONQUEST AND ITS AFTERMATH

DEFENCE was a reserved subject under both dyarchy and the constitution of 1937, so that up to the time of the Japanese invasion the defence of Burma was a British responsibility. In normal times the military forces at the disposal of the Government consisted of two battalions of British infantry, three of Indian infantry, the so-called Burma Rifles, a company of sappers and miners and ten battalions of military police. Karens, Chins and Kachins composed the bulk of the armed forces actually recruited in Burma. During the World War of 1914–1918 Burmans had been enlisted in units from their country which gave good service in Mesopotamia, Palestine and France. But in 1925 they were discharged from the Burma Rifles. The theory was that they were suited neither to the discipline of a modern army, nor for service in a force which might have to be used against their own fellow-countrymen. A few were admitted into the volunteer Burma Auxiliary Force, and they formed the bulk of the University Training Corps; but on leaving the university there was little scope for them to put their training to further use. At the outbreak of the Second World War in 1939 the Burma Defence Force contained only 472 Burmans as against 3197 Karens, Chins and Kachins.

Although the possibility of Japan entering the field as the opponent of the British Commonwealth was fully realized, danger to Burma was not anticipated, since it was assumed that she was sufficiently protected by Singapore. When the Japanese destroyed this comfortable illusion by approaching Burma through French Indo-China and Siam, it was too late to raise and train a Burmese army strong enough to be of any use. The fall of France in June 1940 provided Japan with the opportunity she had previously lacked of attacking Singapore by the back door. When in December 1941, three days after Pearl Harbour, the *Prince of Wales* and the *Repulse* were sunk in the Gulf of

Siam, Japan attained naval supremacy in the Pacific and East
Asiatic waters.

Nearly six months earlier, with Vichy's complicity, she had
gained control over French Indo-China. It was a simple
matter therefore to bring about the capitulation of Pibul
Songgram's government in Bangkok (8 December, 1941). Siam
thus became a threat to Burma well before the fall of Singapore.
But against land attack by a modern power the country was
defenceless. It had neither strategic roads nor railways to its
threatened frontier. No additional troops were stationed there,
and it possessed no munitions factories. Under the circumstances only decisive air superiority could have saved it; but
there was the same lack of aircraft as caused the loss of Hong
Kong, Malaya and Singapore in rapid succession. Adequate
reinforcements of troops could not be spared for Burma because the Japanese invaded simultaneously with their thrust
through Malaya against Singapore, and it was upon the latter
that the British concentrated almost their whole attention.

The Japanese attacked with specially-trained veteran
troops. Against these at first the British could muster only two
under-strength divisions, untrained in meeting Japanese
tactics and provided with equipment quite unsuitable for
jungle warfare. These were supported by a handful of R.A.F
and R.I.A.F. planes, strengthened by the gallant American
Volunteer Group, whose exploits only served to demonstrate
all the more clearly how different the result might have been,
had air superiority been on the British side.

The invasion began in the third week of January 1942 with
two thrusts into Tenasserim, the northern through the Kaw-
kereik Pass debouching into the Moulmein plain, the southern
from Victoria Point towards Mergui. The British made their
first stand on the Salween river around Moulmein. Thence
they were driven westwards along the coast road through
Thaton and across the Sittang to Pegu. A second defeat there
led to the evacuation of Rangoon and a retreat on Prome.
Unable to hold this place, they began to fight a rearguard
action up the Irrawaddy.

Meanwhile Chinese help, under the command of the
American General Stilwell, flowed in over the Burma Road.

The Fifth and Sixth Chinese armies took up a position at Pyawbwe, sent detachments on to Toungoo, and made an attempt to co-operate with the British in holding a line running across the country from Pyinmana to Allanmyo. The Japanese, however, foiled this by driving a wedge between the British and the Chinese. The British thereupon fell back up the Chindwin valley towards Manipur. Crossing the river at Kalewa they made their way up the Kabaw Valley to Tamu and thence over the Naga Hills to Imphal. Stilwell, retreating from Pyinmana, hoped to make a stand in northern Burma, but the Japanese prevented this by piercing the Shan Hills and defeating a Chinese force at Loilem. Stilwell with a mixed band of Americans, British, Burmese and Chinese trekked off towards India through Banmauk, and crossed the Chindwin at Homalin. The remainder of the Chinese armies disintegrated.

The Japanese had conquered Burma with only four divisions. They now began to build up their strength for an attack on India. To meet this the Allies had at first no co-ordinated plan. In the dry weather of 1942–43 a British attempt to seize northern Arakan failed disastrously. The Americans were all for re-opening the land route to China and a drive to secure Myitkyina. The British were sceptical of a North Burma offensive but ultimately yielded to American pressure. The Americans therefore began feverishly to construct the Ledi Road and at the same time to supply China with Lease-Lend materials by air over the Himalayan Hump.

Early in 1943 a co-ordinated plan emerged, which envisaged a drive for Myitkyina by Stilwell's force, a push across the Chindwin from Manipur by the main Allied army, and the despatch of Wingate's specially-trained 'Chindit' force to operate behind the Japanese lines without any communications save by air. In the spring of that year Wingate's small force, composed of British, Burmese and Gurkha troops, marched across Burma from Tonhe on the Chindwin to the Mandalay-Myitkyina railway. Unfortunately the complementary operations had to be cancelled, and the Chindits' campaign of sabotage and destruction lost much of its purpose and meaning, save as a heartening demonstration of heroism.

At the Quebec Conference in August 1943 a big step

forward was taken by the formation of a South-East Asia Command with Mountbatten as Supreme Commander and Stilwell as Deputy Chief. Operation Capital for the recovery of Burma was then worked out on the lines of the existing plan, though on a much larger scale. At the end of the year a second attempt on northern Arakan was made, but it was stopped by a Japanese counter-attack early in 1944. Meanwhile the Japanese had begun to realize that the Allies were making formidable preparations for a large-scale invasion of Burma. To disrupt this they launched a great attack on Manipur and Assam in March of 1944. Their first objective was Imphal, the capture of which would afford them a stepping-off ground for an invasion of Bengal. They hoped also in this way to isolate Stilwell, who was poised in the far north for his drive against Myitkyina, and to render fruitless any second attempt by Wingate's Chindits to operate in the interior.

The attack on Manipur began early in March while Stilwell was moving towards the Hukawng Valley. At almost the same time Wingate led a far more powerful expedition, this time airborne, which sought to paralyse Japanese resistance to Stilwell's advance. For some months the situation was critical, with the Japanese besieging Imphal and striking at Kohima in a desperate attempt to reach Dimapur Junction on the Assam railway, along which most of Stilwell's supplies had to pass.

It was a veritable bloodbath. By the end of June, however, the Japanese were firmly held, and the road from Kohima to Imphal had been cleared. This was the turn of the tide. Inside northern Burma Stilwell's group with the co-operation of the Chindits was relentlessly pressing towards Myitkyina which fell at the end of August. Unfortunately Wingate, the brilliant leader of the Chindits, lost his life in an air accident early in the campaign, and Stilwell, through differences with Chiang Kai-shek, was relieved of his command after the fall of Myitkyina. But by this time the Japanese were in disorderly retreat from Imphal, and the Allied invasion of central Burma was about to begin in earnest.

The cold season of 1944 saw a third Arakan campaign, which cleared the Japanese from the Kaladan Valley and the Mayu peninsula. Then in January 1945 landings from the sea were made at Akyab and other places on the coast, so that the essential forward airfields might be prepared ready for co-operation with the land invasion of Lower Burma. Soon afterwards central Burma was invaded. The leading feature of this operation was the masterly advance of General Slim's Fourteenth Army down the Chindwin to Mandalay and Meiktila. Mandalay fell in March. At the beginning of April the Japanese were heavily defeated at Meiktila and their armies began to disintegrate. Some melted into the Shan Hills eastward, others tried to get away southward across the Sittang, while their Twenty-eighth Army in Arakan began hurriedly moving out by the An and Taungup passes.

It was at this juncture that the Burma National Army went over to the Allies. The Burmese as a whole had given no support to the Japanese at the beginning of the war. The criminal classes, some hundreds of previous rebels and gangs of rowdies had run wild, robbed and looted their own people and murdered Indian refugees. They were formed into the Burma Independence Army by thirty young Burmese nationalists who had been trained on the notorious Hainan Island. But this force was more of an embarrassment than help to the Japanese, and they were ultimately forced to disband it. Later, under Dr. Ba Maw's 'independent' Government of Burma a national service corps was established, which in time became the Burma National Army, officered mainly by Burmese under the close supervision of Japanese experts. It was this force which after lengthy clandestine negotiations with Mountbatten changed sides as the Allied forces advanced swiftly down the Irrawaddy and the Sittang valleys.

The advance now became a race. Prome was occupied before the Japanese Arakan army had extricated itself from the passes across the Arakan Yoma; and its main escape route was thus sealed. Pegu was reached on 1 May and on the following day Rangoon. The advance had been so swift that the plan for a sea-born assault on Rangoon was rendered unnecessary.

One more major operation only had to be fought, the 'battle of the break-through' against 10,000 Japanese, whom General Koba collected in the Pegu Yoma from the remnants of the armies moving out of Arakan and from the west of the

Prome-Rangoon road. It took place in the latter part of July. Thereafter it was only a matter of stamping out the resistance of outlying Japanese garrisons and chasing their retreating forces through the Shan Hills towards Siam. While these measures were in progress atom bombs were dropped on Hiroshima and Nagasaki and Japan surrendered. Soon afterwards General Kimura, the Japanese commander in Burma, signalled Mountbatten that he had ordered the cease-fire.

Burma has been called 'Britain's principal shop window in the war against Japan'. Seen as a whole, the battle for Burma was the largest single action fought against the Japanese. To the Allies its importance lay in the maintenance of communications with China, and in the Japanese threat to India, which envisaged a possible link-up between their armies and the Germans. But the Japanese invasion of India in 1944 was not a serious attempt at conquest; it came two years too late, when the allies were gathering strength, and Japan herself was so fully extended that she could barely maintain her conquests in South-East Asia. It aimed merely at hindering the Allies from making their inevitable counter-attack. Japan's entry into World War II had been a huge gamble, which depended upon Germany's success; against this background only can the Burma campaigns be seen in their true perspective.

The Japanese occupation of Burma wrecked the country's economic system. Burma suffered more from the war than any other Asiatic country save possibly Japan herself. Many of her towns were reduced to ashes by Japanese air-raids. Her oil works, mines equipment and river transport were destroyed by the retreating British so as to be useless to the enemy. Allied air-raids kept her railways out of action. The Japanese systematically looted the country of machinery, scientific apparatus and even furniture. All her normal external markets were lost. The complete stoppage of her rice export, through the failure of the Japanese to take it, led to mere subsistence farming. The south suffered from a glut of rice while the dry zone starved. Lower Burma was almost completely deprived of the cooking oil which only the dry zone could supply. The failure of the Japanese to export Burma rice and import urgently needed consumer goods caused the greatest distress, which was further aggravated by the chaos and uncontrollable inflation caused by the Japanese currency policy. The Burmese had to comply with the very heavy demands of the Japanese for forced labour while frightful atrocities were committed upon the Karens, who had hidden British soldiers and formed European-led resistance groups.

Administration was at first handed over to the Burma Independence Army. After its suppression a Burmese Executive Administration was set up in August 1942 with Dr. Ba Maw at its head. Under it many officers of the old civil administration resumed duty. Under Japanese sponsorship Burma's 'independence' was proclaimed on 1 August, 1943. The constitution of 1937 was swept away, Ba Maw became the 'Adipadi', the Pali equivalent of *Führer*, and a *gauleiter* was appointed to each district. Real control, however, was in the hands of Dr. Gotara Ogawa, formerly Minister of Commerce and Railways in Tokyo, who was named 'Supreme Adviser' to the Burmese Government. The nominal independence thus accorded was at first accepted by many Burmans as the genuine article. They were not long in discovering that the propagandist talk about Asiatic brotherhood and co-prosperity was merely a cloak for ruthless exploitation. Hence the return of the British was hailed with joy, and the Burma National Army played a useful part in mopping-up operations against the retreating Japanese.

Its leader, Aung San, became the focus of nationalist aspirations, which found expression in a political organization known as the Anti-Fascist People's Freedom League. Aung San had sprung to fame as the organizer of the students' strike of 1936. Thereafter he had become the leader of the *thakin* group, a small party of extremists, who called themselves by the name of respect accorded to Europeans, and equivalent to *sahib* in India. He had fled to Japan in 1940, and with others of his party had accompanied the Japanese when they invaded Burma. In Ba Maw's cabinet he was Minister for Defence, and together with Than Tun, the Minister for Transport and Supply, had secretly organized the anti-Japanese swing of the Burma National Army. It was a move demanding courage, ability and discipline. Its success made Aung San and his A.F.P.F.L. the most potent political force in the country when British administration was restored. He profited from the fact that the older political leaders of pre-war days were discredited in the eyes of the people as corrupt and self-seeking. The A.F.P.F.L. was a union of no less than ten political groups, including the Communists, and was supported by the Arakanese, Karens and Shans as well as by the overwhelming mass of the Burmese.

Such was the situation when civil government was officially restored in October 1945. Right from the start the professed aim of Aung San and his party was complete independence. Dominion Status had little appeal for them. They had a deep distrust of British motives, and feared that Burma was once more to be made the happy hunting-ground of British business interests. Nevertheless they realized their need of British assistance, capital and expert knowledge.

British policy at first envisaged a reconstruction period of some years as a preparation for the long-promised grant of Dominion Status. In October 1946, however, after an organized strike of police and government officials, Aung San and the other A.F.P.F.L. leaders won their way into the Governor's Executive Council. Up to that moment they had accepted the co-operation of the Communists. On attaining power they were compelled to view the problems of government from the practical angle of the maintenance of law and order, the achievement of economic stability, and the establishment of public confidence. Hence they had to break with their old allies, whose outlook and methods were soon found to be not in accord with the true national aspirations of the people.

This move made it possible for Britain to view their demands with greater sympathy, and when in January 1947 Aung San came to London to discuss matters with Attlee's Labour Cabinet, an agreement was signed whereby his government was granted control over Burma's finances and army, and the right to hold a general election for a Constituent Assembly in the following April. The British Government bound itself to accept the verdict of the Burma electorate even if the result were a vote in favour of complete independence.

The agreement, however, was subject to one overruling proviso which safeguarded the rights of the other indigenous races of Burma, the Karens, Shans, Kachins and Chins, who were by no means anxious to come under direct Burmese control. At the subsequent election Aung San won a resounding victory. At the same time he managed to allay the hostility of the Hill Peoples by practically allowing them to write their own terms into the new constitution. The Karens alone, with the memory still fresh of their cruel treatment at the hands of the Burma Independence Army, remained unsatisfied, and somewhat unrealistically stood out for a state of their own, sublimely ignoring the fact that with the majority of them living in the Irrawaddy and Tenasserim divisions, inextricably mixed with the Burmese, such a solution was impossible. Aung San, it must be admitted, did his utmost to meet all their more reasonable claims with statesmanlike patience and understanding.

The Burma Constituent Assembly completed its work and unanimously passed the new constitution on 24 September, 1947. But by that time Aung San was no more. On 19 July, 1947, he and several of his colleagues were assassinated at a Cabinet meeting by ruffians in the pay of a political rival. The leadership of the A.F.P.F.L. and of the Government passed into the hands of Thakin Nu, whose policy was in all essentials the same as the dead leader's.

The Assembly's decision was in favour of complete independence, and in mid-October Thakin Nu came to London to negotiate Burma's secession from the British Commonwealth. The outcome was the signature on 17 October, 1947, of the treaty recognizing the Republic of the Union of Burma as a fully independent state on a date to be fixed by Parliament. A Burma Independence Bill was accordingly passed through Parliament and on 4 January, 1948, Sir Hubert Rance, the last British Governor, handed over charge to the Republic's first President, a Shan Chieftain, the Sawbwa of Yawnghwe, Sao Shwe Thaik.

What was the cause of the decision to leave the Commonwealth? Many people refuse to believe that Burma really wanted to go, but are of opinion that political propaganda had got to such a pitch that it was impossible to withdraw a demand that had been made so insistently. The Burmese have often been called the 'Irish of the East'. Certainly sentiment weighs far more with them than reason. Their awakening nationalism in the twentieth century made them more acutely conscious than any other people in the East of their long history as an independent power.

But the decision was made in far too much of a hurry; dominion status within the British Commonwealth would have been the wiser solution, and might have been Burma's own choice, if only some way could have been found of deferring a decision until the people had had a better opportunity of learning what was really involved. Britain's attitude was not, as has been somewhat irresponsibly asserted, the result of post-war military and economic weakness. It sprang from a genuine desire to retain the friendship of the Burmese people. One of the most noteworthy features of British administration, too often overlooked by its critics, was the real understanding and friendship, which, individually, Britons and Burmese have always shown towards each other.

The Burmese desire for national independence was natural and inevitable. It took some at least of its inspiration from the system of education introduced by the British themselves. We taught them our language, our literature, our history and our political philosophy, all of which are steeped in the principles of freedom and popular self-government. Through such a medium, and through personal contacts with British teachers, have their best minds learnt to study the problems of the modern world.

CHAPTER XX

THE UNION OF BURMA

THE constitution of the new state placed the supreme executive power in the hands of a Prime Minister and Cabinet responsible to a Chamber of Deputies composed of 250 members, elected by adult suffrage and representing single-member constituencies on a non-communal basis. The second house of the legislature, called the Chamber of Nationalities, was so constituted that a majority of its 125 members represented the non-Burmese peoples of the Union. The constitution provided for the establishment of separate constituent states for the Shans, the Kachins, the Karens and the Karenni states, and of a special division for the Chins. In practice each of these component parts of the Union was represented in the Cabinet. So anxious indeed were the Burmese leaders to conciliate these peoples that they inserted into the constitution a clause of doubtful wisdom granting a constituent state the right of secession by plebiscite after the lapse of ten years from the date of the coming into force of the constitution.

The Karen question called for the most tactful handling. Their separate state, provided for in the constitution, was to be centred in the Salween district, but they were dissatisfied with its extent and powers. The Regional Autonomy Inquiry Commission, charged with the task of forming it, granted their reasonable demands but rejected claims to territory where they constituted only a minority of the population. The negotiations were protracted, and while they were in progress Burma was plunged into chaos by a communist revolt. Then in January 1949, when their leaders were within sight of agreement with the Union government, an attempt to disarm the Karens caused them also to rebel; and, to complete the tragedy, they accepted an offer of support from the communists.

The difficulties accompanying the transfer of power by Britain to Burma, namely the immediate retirement of most British officials and the government's efforts to demilitarize

and resettle thousands of young men in the Burma National
Army, not to mention the economic weakness of the country,
provided the communists with an opportunity to revolt. The
decision was taken at the South-East Asian Communist
Conference, held in Calcutta in February 1948. It marked the
changeover to a more offensive policy throughout eastern
Asia. By themselves the communists had no hope of success.
Their revolt, however, gained support from the so-called
White Band PVOs, remnants of the Burma National Army,
who had originally been organized by Aung San into the
People's Volunteer Organization, and held in readiness to
fight if the negotiations for independence failed. Having no
raison d'être in the new Burma of 1948, and composed of
young men with no training or inclination for civil life, they
constituted a serious problem. They split into two sections
known respectively as White Band and Yellow Band PVOs,
the latter loyal to the government. Nu's efforts to disband
them caused the Whites to go over to the communists.

Had it not been for the Karen rising the communist
rebellion would have been for all practical purposes stamped
out in 1949. But the Karen rising, formidable in itself, all the
more so since it began at Insein close to Rangoon, gave new
life to the communist struggle. Under the terms of their
agreement the KNDOs (Karen National Defence Organization)
were to control Lower Burma, the communists Upper Burma.
In the critical year 1949, when communism triumphed in
China, the rebels captured such key places as Mandalay,
Meiktila, Bassein and Toungoo, and paralysed road, rail and
river communications throughout most of the country.

But the government did not fall, and its determination to
become master in its own house never wavered. U Nu, a
sincere and devoted Buddhist, constantly did his utmost to
prevent bloodshed and promote conciliation; but when at his
instance the Karens agreed to a temporary truce for negotiations, he flatly rejected a settlement on the basis of an
autonomous Karen state with its own army.

It was a slow process winning back the country district
by district, and opening up communications, with the rebels
launching constant counterattacks and often regaining lost

territory. Slowly the tide turned against the insurgents. In
1951, it was possible to hold the first general election after
independence, though only on a regional basis. Voting began
in June in 75 out of the 250 constituencies. By the end of the
year it was practically completed for the whole country, and
over 40 per cent of the electorate went to the polls. They
gave the AFPFL a clear majority. In that year the railway
from Rangoon to Mandalay began to run again for the first
time since 1948.

Early in 1952 the Regional Autonomy Inquiry Commission
completed its work. It recommended that to the original
nucleus of the Karen state in the Salween district adjoining
territories might be added by plebiscite in two stages, though
subject to the restoration of law and order. Accordingly in the
following September a legislative act was passed establishing
a Karen State Government with its own secretariat and a
Karen State Council with legislative competence.

Again the rebellion was on the point of collapse, and again
a complicating factor intervened to give it a fresh lease of
life. In January 1950 the last Kuomintang division on the
Asian mainland, under General Li Mi, was routed in southern
Yunnan by the Chinese communists. Soon afterwards the
remnant of its troops to the number of 10,000, in civilian
dress, began to filter through the Burma border into the Wa
states and Kengtung. Burmese troops attacked the KMTs but
they escaped in small parties into northern Siam, and later
returned. With most of their effective units engaged in dealing
with their own rebels the Burmese found it impossible to deal
effectively with Li Mi, who was obviously receiving a stream
of money, supplies and recruits through Siam, besides levying
'tribute' on the local people. Indeed, following on a request to
the United States in May 1951 to bring pressure on the KMT
regime in Formosa to withdraw Li Mi and his force, Dean
Rusk, the Assistant Secretary of State, made a speech which
seemed to suggest that the Nationalist general had American
support.

During that summer Li Mi failed badly in an invasion of
Yunnan, and at the end of the year his force was in such straits
that it would have disintegrated, had he not received very

substantial aid. It came from Formosa through an independent
American agency in Bangkok. The wildest rumours flew around,
and in January 1952 Mr. Vyshinsky in the United Nations
Assembly charged the American Command with the transfer
of troops from Formosa to Siam and eastern Burma. No
evidence, however, has ever been produced of America's
official complicity in what had now become a very dirty
business.

Throughout 1952 Li Mi was building up his strength in
defiance of Burma. Early in 1953 his units launched attacks
across the Salween into the Shan State, the Kachin State and
the Kayah State (Karenni). So, instead of completing the task
of crushing her rebels, Burma had to use the major part of her
armed forces in driving off the invaders. In April 1953 she took
the matter to the United Nations General Assembly, asking
that effective measures should be taken to compel the evacuation of the KMT forces. The upshot of this was an agreement
by Chiang Kai-shek's government to negotiate. After months
of deliberate prevarication a sham evacuation was carried out
during November and December 1953. The Burma army
thereupon launched a major offensive, 'Operation Bayinnaung',
which culminated in the capture of the KMT headquarters
in March 1954. Even then, although a further evacuation
was agreed upon, thousands of Li Mi's forces were never
rounded up, and today still prey upon the hill villages of
Kengtung.

It was the turn of the rebels next. In July 1954 a drive
against the communists in central Burma destroyed them as
an effective force, while another against the PVOs was equally
successful. The Karen National Defence Organization was the
toughest nut to crack. Determined operations against them in
the Delta region and on the Siam border towards the end of
1953 broke the back of their resistance. The final blow, however,
was not delivered until March 1955 when Papun their 'capital'
was captured. The rebellions have now all been crushed, but
at the time of writing (Autumn 1955) lawlessness and dacoity
still remain very serious problems.

In its first flush of enthusiasm the AFPFL drew up a
comprehensive programme of nationalization. Land in par-

ticular was to be nationalized, while the development of Burma's natural resources was to be carried out by companies in which Burmese citizens owned at least 60 per cent of the stock. With a painful deficiency of technicians, and ministers without the experience for administering a socialized state, the implementation of such a programme was bound to have encountered insurmountable obstacles, even had disorder and rebellion not imposed a decisive check upon internal development projects.

Thus the undue hurry to nationalize the Irrawaddy Flotilla Company and the dismissal of most of its foreign engineers had disastrous results, while the first land nationalization scheme, attempted in the Syriam District, broke down so completely that for some years afterwards little was done in this sphere. With the oil companies the original arrangement, whereby the Union government with the aid of a loan from Britain was to purchase over a lengthy period a controlling interest, and the companies were to train Burmans for their higher posts, was abandoned.

On the other hand in 1951 the Burma Corporation was successfully reconstituted as a joint venture between the former company and the government of the Union on a fifty-fifty basis. The actual management of the mineral properties at Bawdwin and Namtu with their related hydro-electric plant and railroad was left with the company under an arrangement providing for intensive Burmanization and eventual nationalization as soon as financial circumstances should permit. In that same year negotiations began again with the oil companies for a joint venture on the basis of the companies owning two-thirds and the government one-third of the capital, and of an immediate rehabilitation programme restricted to restarting the Chauk refinery.

With the passing of the most dangerous phase of disorder land nationalization gained a new urgency, largely because of the stress laid upon it by communist propaganda. Hence in 1952 a Ministry of Land Nationalization was created, and in 1953 and 1954 new legislation was passed amending the original Land Nationalization Act of 1948 in the light of the lessons learnt in attempting to put it into practice. The work of distribution was entrusted to elected village councils; the aim was to promote a system of co-operative farming. The results so far attained show that sitting tenants have been confirmed in their holdings and owner-cultivators exempted from nationalization, and, moreover, the old pattern of farming remains unchanged. Expropriated landlords, however, have not yet received their promised compensation.

In the pre-war period British administrators had failed to solve the problem of agricultural indebtedness and the dominance of the non-agricultural non-resident Indian land-lord. The reason was largely because until 'separation' in 1937 Burma had been a province of India, and even after 1937 India remained the senior partner in a close economic relationship with Burma. When the Japanese entered Burma, some 500,000 Indians fled the country, and in the absence of the chettyar landlords the Burmese tenants took over their lands. Ba Maw's government legalized the existing state of affairs, and the Burmese cultivator saw his burden of debt as it were miraculously removed.

After the war, even before the transfer of sovereignty, legislation was passed which aimed at preventing once and for all a recurrence of the pre-war situation. Under a Land Alienation Act, a Rent Control Act and a Disposal of Tenancies Act the peasant obtained the maximum possible security. The Land Nationalization Act, passed after independence, pro-hibited the holding of land by non-agriculturists. It was also made illegal to transfer immovable property to an alien for more than a year.

The provisions in the Land Nationalization Act for the payment of compensation to dispossessed landlords, bitterly denounced by the communists, who would pay none, were considered ruinously inadequate by the chettyars in India, who were the legal owners of three million acres of Burma paddy land, and had managed to preserve their title deeds when they fled. Pressure from the Government of India on their behalf failed to move the Burmese. Indeed, the Union government was in no mood to consider large payments of compensation; for one thing it was itself accumulating an increasing burden of bad debts as a result of its lavish distribution of agricultural loans. In 1951 it wrote off Rs. 109 millions' worth of them. The chettis made unofficial approaches to both Rangoon and New Delhi, but in vain. Happily, however, the close friendship of Pandit Nehru and U Nu ensured the maintenance of good relations between their two countries. The Government of India made a generous settlement of its economic claims on Burma, and Nehru let it be known that while Burma's proposals for compensation for nationalized land had caused 'considerable distress', there would be no interference in what was the entire concern of the Burmese government. Nevertheless, the shedding of the Indian money-lender and the expropriation of the landlord have by no means solved the thorny problem of agricultural credit.

Throughout the early difficult years of the Union, when valuable pre-war sources of revenue such as oil, minerals and timber yielded nothing, the export of rice saved it from bank-ruptcy. The price of rice in the world market was so favourable that notwithstanding $2\frac{1}{2}$ million acres of paddy land lying waste, a shortage of plough cattle and much disorder, the government was more than able to pay its way through its control over rice exports. Its State Agricultural Marketing Board bought rice from the cultivator at £10 a ton and sold it abroad at prices which rose from £40 a ton in 1949 to between £60 and £70 a ton in the first half of 1953.

In June 1953, however, a steady weakening of world rice prices began, and gradually caused mounting difficulties for Burma. She had to reduce her prices very heavily, even those regulated under long-term agreements. And at the very moment when her ambitious Welfare State programme, set forth at the Pyidawtha Conference in August 1952, was entering its most expensive phase, her monetary reserves were rapidly melting away. By the middle of 1955 they had fallen to one-third of what they had been two years earlier.

Colombo Plan assistance was on altogether too small a scale to affect this situation. American aid had been cancelled by Burma when she took the KMT affair to the United Nations. Hence, with unsold rice on her hands, she had anxiously to search for new markets. In November 1954 she concluded a barter deal with China, and a further one in the following March. Japan, shorn of her Manchurian supply, was also willing to increase her purchases of Burma rice. But perhaps the most significant step towards finding the money to finance her Pyidawtha programme was the reparations agreement concluded by Burma with Japan in September 1954. It provided that Japan should pay $200 million over a period of ten years in the form of capital goods and services, and invest a further $50 million in 'joint enterprises' in Burma.

Right from the start U Nu saw that the success of Burma as a small independent state was bound up with the maintenance of world peace. He espoused Pandit Nehru's neutralist policy and scrupulously kept clear of any commitment which might identify Burma with either of the great power blocs of the post-war world. Then, as he gained confidence through increasing contacts with political leaders in other countries, he adopted a more positive policy, based upon the cultivation of good relations with China. Thus in July 1954 Chou En-lai paid a visit to Burma, and in the following December Nu visited Peking. This closer relationship involved no weakening in Nu's attitude towards the communist insurgents in his own country. Indeed, both statesmen were thoroughly realist in their dealings with each other. From then onwards Nu has gained no little authority in international affairs, and his many journeyings in 1955 have played a real part in lessening tension in eastern Asia.

Fundamentally Nu's moral strength stems from his deep religious convictions. In his youth he felt the impact of the Buddhist revival which was so prominent a feature of the nationalist movement against British rule. Through his efforts it reached a culminating point in 1954 with the gathering of the Sixth Buddhist Council in world history, charged with the task of reciting and examining the whole of the Pali scriptures. The idealist in Nu believes in the saving grace of Buddhism. It is his spiritual weapon against the onslaught of dialectical materialism. Still more, he hopes that through this public restatement of Buddhist truths the hearts of men everywhere will be inclined to peace.

SELECT BIBLIOGRAPHY

(*a*) BIBLIOGRAPHY:

The most comprehensive bibliography of writings on Burma is in the late J. L. Christian's

Burma and the Japanese Invader (Bombay, 1945), which is an enlarged edition of his previous *Modern Burma* (University of California Press, 1942).

(*b*) STANDARD WORKS:

There are only two standard histories in English, both out of print and scarce:

Phayre, Sir Arthur Purves: *History of Burma.* (London, 1883.)

Harvey, G. E.: *History of Burma from the Earliest Times to the Beginning of the English Conquest.* (London, 1925.)

In Burmese the standard chronicles, together covering the whole period up to 1885, are:

The Hmannan Yazawin. (Mandalay, 1908.)

The Konbaungset Chronicle. (Mandalay, 1905.)

There is an excellent English translation of the earlier portions of the former by G. H. Luce and Pe Maung Tin, entitled *The Glass Palace Chronicle of the Kings of Burma.* (London, 1923.)

There are two major collections of inscriptions:

Duroiselle, C., and Blagden, C. O.: *Epigraphia Birmanica.* 5 vols. (Rangoon, 1919–36.)

Luce, G. H., and Pe Maung Tin: *Inscriptions of Burma.* 3 portfolios. (Other portfolios in preparation.) (London, 1933–39.)

(*c*) CONTEMPORARY ACCOUNTS:

The most important contemporary accounts by European visitors are:

(i) Caesar Frederick's and Ralph Fitch's in Richard Hakluyt's *Principall Navigations*,

(ii) the journals of Edward Fleetwood, George Baker, Robert Lester and Walter Alves in Alexander Dalrymple's *Oriental Repertory* (London, 1808), a reprint of the Burma portions of which was published in Rangoon in 1926, and

(iii) the following works separately published:

Cox, Captain Hiram: *Journal of a Residence in the Burmhan Empire.* (London, 1821.)

Crawfurd, John: *Journal of an Embassy to the Court of Ava in the Year 1827.* (London, 1829.)

Francklin, W.: *Tracts, Political, Geographical and Commercial, on the Dominions of Ava and the North-Western Parts of Hindostaun.* (London, 1811.)

Gouger, H.: *Personal Narrative of Two Years' Imprisonment in Burmah.* (London, 1860.)

Hunter, W.: *A Concise Account of the Kingdom of Pegu.* (Calcutta and London, 1789.)

Sangermano, Father: *A Description of the Burmese Empire.* (Rangoon, 1885.)

Symes, Michael: *An Account of an Embassy to the Kingdom of Ava.* (London, 1800.)

Yule, Sir Henry: *A Narrative of the Mission sent by the Governor-General of India to the Court of Ava in 1855.* (London, 1858.)

(d) MONOGRAPHS AND SPECIAL STUDIES:

Anderson, John: *Mandalay to Momein.* (London, 1876.)

Andrus, J. R.: *Burmese Economic Life.* (Stanford (U.S.A.) and London, 1948.)

Aung, Maung Htin: *Burmese Drama: A Study with Translations of Burmese Plays.* (London, 1937.)

Clifford, Sir Hugh: *Further India.* (London, 1904.)

Cœdès, G.: *Les États Hindouisés d'Indochine et d'Indonésie.* (Paris, 1948.)

Collis, Maurice: *Siamese White.* (London, 1935.)

—— *The Land of the Great Image.* (London, 1943.)

Colquhoun, Archibald R.: *Across Chryse.* 2 vols. (London, 1883.)

Colquhoun, A. R., and Hallett, Holt S.: *Report on the Railway Connection of Burmah and China.* (London, undated, 1887.)?

Crossthwaite, Sir Charles: *The Pacification of Burma.* (London, 1912.)

Desai, W. S.: *History of the British Residency in Burma, 1826–1840.* (Rangoon, 1939.)

Furnivall, J. S.: *Colonial Policy and Practice. A Comparative Study of Burma and Netherlands India.* (Cambridge, 1948.)

—— *An Introduction to the Political Economy of Burma.* (Rangoon, 1931.)

Fytche, Sir Albert: *Burma Past and Present.* 2 vols. (London, 1878.)

Grousset, R., Auboyer, J., and Buhot, J.: *L'Asie Orientale des Origins au XVᵉ Siècle.* (Paris, 1941.)

Hall, D. G. E.: *Early English Intercourse with Burma, 1587–1743.* (London, 1928.)

—— *The Dalhousie-Phayre Correspondence, 1852–56.* (London, 1932.)

—— *Europe and Burma, A Study of European Relations with Burma to the Annexation of Thibaw's Kingdom, 1886.* (London, 1945.)

Hall, H. Fielding: *The Soul of a People.* (London, 1926.)

Harvey, G. E.: *British Rule in Burma, 1824–1942.* (London, 1946.)

Ireland, Alleyne: *The Province of Burma.* 2 vols. (New York, 1907.)

Labourdonnais, Le Comte A. Mahé de: *Un Français en Birmanie* (Paris, 1891.)

Laurie, W. F. B.: *Our Burmese Wars and Relations with Burma.* (London, 1885.)

Lehault, P. (Frederic Haas): *La France et l'Angleterre en Asie.* (Paris, 1892.)

Mason, Rev. F.: *Burma, its People and Productions.* (Hertford, U.S.A., 1882.)

McKelvie, R.: *The War in Burma.* (London, 1948.)

Mitton, G. E. (Lady Scott): *Scott of the Shan Hills.* (London, 1885.)

Nisbet, J.: *Burmah under British Rule and Before.* (London, 1901.)

Parker, E. H.: *Burma, with Special Reference to her Relations with China.* (Rangoon, 1893.)

Pearn, B. R.: *History of Rangoon.* (Rangoon, 1939.)

Ray, N. R.: *Sanskrit Buddhism in Burma.* (Calcutta, 1936.)

Report of the Provincial Enquiry Committee on Vernacular and Vocational Education. (Rangoon, 1936.)

Report of the Riots Enquiry Committee. (Rangoon, 1939.)

Report on the Administration of Burma. (Rangoon, annually to 1936.)

Report of the Burma Provincial Banking Enquiry Committee. 2 vols. (Rangoon, 1930.)

Scott, Sir J. G.: *Burma from the Earliest Times to the Present Day.* (London, 1924.)

—— *The Burman, His Life and Notions.* (London, 1910.)

—— *Burma: A Handbook of Practical Information.* (Edinburgh, 1906.)

Sein, Ma Mya: *Administration of Burma.* (Rangoon, 1938.)

Sen, N. C.: *A Peep into Burma Politics, 1917–42.* (Allahabad, 1945.)

Sladen, Major E. B.: *Narrative of the Expedition to Explore the Trade Routes to China via Bhamo.* (Rangoon, 1869.)

Williams, Clement: *Through Burmah to Western China.* (Edinburgh, 1869.)

Wilson, H. H.: *Narrative of the Burmese War in 1824–26*. (London, 1912.)

Wood, W. A. R.: *History of Siam*. (London, 1926.)

(*e*) CONTRIBUTIONS TO THE JOURNAL OF THE BURMA RESEARCH
　　　SOCIETY:

Furnivall, J. S.: "The Fashioning of Leviathan: The Beginnings of British Rule in Burma". (Vol. XXIX, 1939.)

Hall, D. G. E.: "The Tragedy of Negrais". (Vol. XXI, 1931.)

—— "Studies in Dutch Relations with Arakan". (Vol. XXVI, 1936.)

—— "The Daghregister of Batavia and Dutch Relations with Burma in the 17th Century". (Vol. XXIX, 1939.)

Langham-Carter, R. R.: "The Burmese Army". (Vol. XXVII, 1937.)

Luce, G. H.: "Early Chinese Texts about Burma". (Vol. XIV, 1924.)

—— "Burma's Debt to Pagan". (Vol. XXII, 1932.)

—— "The Ancient Pyu". (Vol. XXVII, 1937.)

—— "Burma Down to the Fall of Pagan". (With Pe Maung Tin.) Part I. (Vol. XXIX, 1939.)

—— "The Economic Life of the Early Burman". (Vol. XXX, 1940.)

—— "A Century of Progress in Burmese History and Archaeology". (Vol. XXXII, 1948.)

Pearn, B. R.: "King-bering". (Vol. XXIII, 1933.)

Stewart, J. A.: "Some Authorities for the History of Burma". (Vol. XIII, 1923.)

INDEX

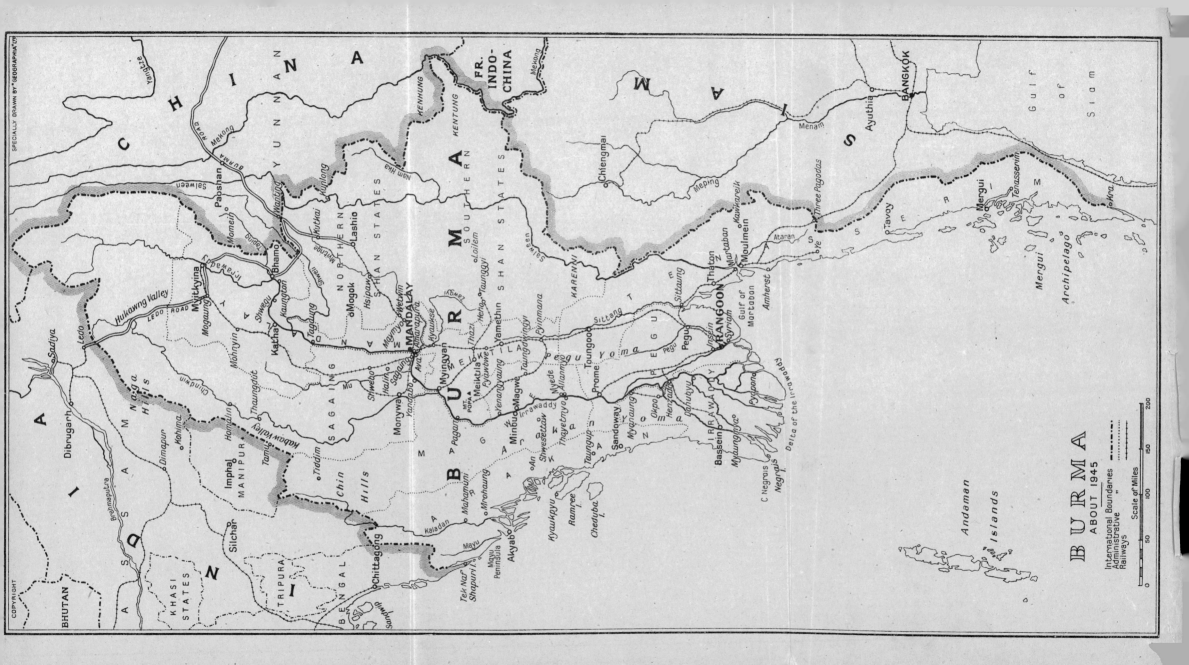

BURMA
ABOUT 1945

International Boundaries
Administrative
Railways

Scale of Miles

0   50   100   150   200

SPECIALLY DRAWN BY "GEOGRAPHIA" LTD
COPYRIGHT

CHINA

YUNNAN

FR. INDO-CHINA

SIAM

BANGKOK

Gulf of Siam

BURMA

NORTHERN SHAN STATES

SOUTHERN SHAN STATES

KENTUNG

KENHUNG

Mekong

Salween

Yangtze

Paoshan

Momein

Bhamo

Myitkyina

Mogaung

Ledo

Sadiya

Dibrugarh

Hukawng Valley

LEDO ROAD

BURMA ROAD

Irrawaddy

Kaungtan

Shwegu

Katha

Tagaung

Mohnyin

Mogok

Hsipaw

Lashio

Kunlong

Wanting

Mutkai

Namtu

Nam Hka

Loilem

Mong Nai

Mandalay

Maymyo

Wetwin

Amarapura

Ava

Sagaing

Shwebo

Halin

Monywa

Yandabo

Pagan

MT. POPA

Myingyan

Kyaukse

Thazi

Meiktila

Pyawbwe

Yamethin

Pyinmana

Toungoo

Pegu

RANGOON

Insein

Syriam

Gulf of Martaban

Martaban

Moulmein

Amherst

Thaton

Sittang

Meping

Chiengmai

Menam

Ayuthia

Three Pagodas

Ataran

Ye

Tavoy

TENASSERIM

Mergui

Mergui Archipelago

Tenasserim

Kra

Andaman Islands

PEGU YOMA

Sittang

Prome

Allanmyo

Thayetmyo

Magwe

Minbu

Yenangyaung

Shwesettaw

Nyede

Okpo

Henzada

Bassein

Myaungmya

Pyapon

Delta of the Irrawaddy

IRRAWADDY

ARAKAN YOMA

Sandoway

Myohaung

Taungup

An

Kyaukpyu

Ramree I.

Cheduba I.

C Negrais

Negrais I.

Mahamuni

Mrohaung

Akyab

Kaladan

Mayu

Mayu Peninsula

Shapuri I.

Tek Naf

Chittagong

BENGAL

TRIPURA

KHASI STATES

BHUTAN

ASSAM

Brahmaputra

Silchar

Dimapur

Kohima

Imphal

MANIPUR

Tamu

Tiddim

Homalin

Thaungdut

Chindwin

NAGA HILLS

Kabow Valley

CHIN HILLS

SAGAING

Chin

Mu